KEEPING YOUR HEART FOR MINISTRY

MICHAEL D. MILLER

LifeWay Press
Nashville, Tennessee

ISBN 0-7673-9453-4

This book is a text for three Christian Growth Study Plan courses.

Dewey Decimal Classification: 253
Subject Heading: MINISTRY\CHURCH WORK

PRINTED IN THE UNITED STATES OF AMERICA

LifeWay Church Resources
a division of LifeWay Christian Resources
of the Southern Baptist Convention
127 Ninth Avenue North
Nashville, Tennessee 37234

TABLE OF CONTENTS

Keeping Your Heart for Ministry

INTRODUCTION TO YOUR STUDY

I believe the most critical need in God's church today is leadership — men and women who will stand up and lead with integrity and who are effective role models for others.

As I travel throughout our country, I hear a cry arise among church members everywhere: "Being a church leader today is so challenging! So many things cause me to become discouraged and lose heart." Others say, "I truly want to be able to put my whole heart in what I do for God's kingdom, but so much seems to be working against me." Some of the concerns they mention are fatigue, burnout, struggle to inspire others to follow, feeling distant from God, lack of appropriate examples to follow, increased demands on time, distractions, and many, many other obstacles. The heart cry is the same, whether it comes from a pastor, a staff leader, a Sunday School or discipleship leader, a Women on Mission group president, a support-group facilitator, a committee chairperson, or any dedicated follower of Christ who serves in some leadership capacity. Being at the helm of a project, a class, a department, or a congregation can be wearying. Although the heavenly rewards are great, the earthly rewards seem few. How can a leader be refreshed and renewed for service?

In this five-week study, *Keeping Your Heart for Ministry*, I want you to discover some practical tips that will give you a fresh outlook on the work God has outlined for you in the service of His kingdom. I write this book as a fellow struggler — one who has encountered many of the same obstacles and heartaches, but also as one who has seen that God's grace is sufficient for any leader who takes advantage of it. In the pages that follow I will share about some of the godly role models who have gone before me, some principles from God's Word that have been lifelines for me, and some of the lessons I've learned in God's school of leadership. My prayer is that this time of study and reflection will help you take significant steps toward growing in faithful leadership in the eyes of Jesus Christ.

The topics for the next five weeks are designed to help you examine key elements in mature Christian leadership:

- Your Heart, Your Ministry
- Keeping Your Heart for God
- Keeping Your Heart for the Kingdom
- Keeping Your Heart for the Church
- Keeping Your Heart for the World

Keeping Your Heart for Ministry can be used in a variety of ways.

- Pastors throughout a city or an association may desire to come together as a group to meet weekly and discuss the workbook concepts.
- A pastor may lead a study for staff members or for the deacon body.
- A missionary might gather key leaders in a new or expanding mission venture.
- A minister of education might want to organize a study for all the Sunday School teachers in his church.
- A church's youth leaders, prayer ministry workers, or any other select group could come together in similar settings.
- The director of a Christian weekday program could use this study with her teaching staff.

Of course, an effective study could be conducted with any combination of those in leadership roles, because the challenge to keep your heart for ministry occurs across the board, regardless of the position held. It could also benefit someone who might be praying about taking on a new leadership responsibility and who wonders how he or she can stay motivated for the task ahead.

Each day, for five days a week, you are asked to study a segment of the material and complete activities that relate to what you just read. Each day's work requires about 20 to 30 minutes of study time. Even if you find that you can study the material in less time, spread out the study over five days. This will give you more time to apply the truths to your life.

INTRODUCTION TO YOUR STUDY *continued . . .*

Members gather for group sessions at the end of each week's study. The sessions help you reflect on the concepts and experiences in *Keeping Your Heart for Ministry* and apply the ideas to your life. You will share insights gained, look for answers to problems encountered, and gain strength from the fact that others are encountering similar struggles and victories. The element of accountability present in a group setting seems to be an essential for life change.

Although you may benefit from completing the study totally on your own without a group experience, you will have missed the critical element Jesus' disciples experienced: relationships with one another in Christ's presence. As members share their own testimonies about growing in awareness of how to keep their hearts for ministry, others give feedback and are encouraged in their own challenges and victories. That is why I strongly recommend that you connect with other believers to study this material.

Study the book as if I were sitting at your side, helping you learn. When I ask you a question or give you an assignment, respond immediately. Each assignment appears in **boldface type.** In most cases, I will give you some feedback about your response — for example, a suggestion about what you might have written. This process is designed to help you learn the material more effectively. Do not deny yourself valuable learning opportunities by skipping the activities.

Set a definite time and select a quiet place where you can study with little interruption. Keep your Bible open for times when the material asks you to look up Scripture. Make notes in the margin of any problems, questions, or concerns that arise as you study. You will discuss many of these during your group sessions.

If you have started a study of *Keeping Your Heart for Ministry* and you are not involved in a group study, try to enlist some friends or associates who will work through this course with you. Husbands and wives who are both involved in leadership roles are encouraged to work through the material together. The *Leader Guide,* at the back of this workbook, provides guidance and learning activities for these sessions.

I pray that God will abundantly bless you with strength and wisdom to undertake this study and with the courage and faith to apply what you learn.

Week 1, Introduction

YOUR HEART, YOUR MINISTRY

This Week

One activity that has become a common part of my life as I have grown older is my annual medical checkup. Not long ago I sat in an examination room discussing with my doctor the results of my physical. He reviewed my chart and then looked at me with a serious expression on his face. What he said shocked me. "I have some bad news for you, Dr. Miller. Your tests reveal that you are 30 pounds overweight, you suffer from high blood pressure, and you are under stress because of your job. In a nutshell, you're a candidate for a heart attack!"

His words hit me like someone had thrown ice water on my head. I began to make excuses. I said to him, "But, Doc, I'm only 40 years old. Surely you are mistaken. You must have picked up someone else's file by accident. I just can't believe what you're telling me." Regardless of how much I fought the report, the facts were true. The tests didn't lie. I was in serious health trouble, no matter how much I tried to deny it.

After listening to my emotional outburst, my physician prescribed several actions that could help me correct my condition. Following his advice would provide me with some means of possibly reducing the risk of a heart attack. At first I refused, protesting, "After all, I'm a preacher. God wouldn't let anything happen to me."

Even while I protested, in my heart I knew the warning signs had surfaced more than once. I brushed them aside, telling myself, "I could lose a few pounds once I put my mind to it." "I'll exercise more once we get these current projects out of the way," I reasoned. The signs were there all right. I'd simply chosen to ignore them.

With a serious yet patient look, my doctor finally responded, "Well, Dr. Miller, it's your life; it's your heart!" I have never forgotten the impact of those words, and I've tried to heed them as I've made some mid-course corrections in some of my lifestyle habits.

Since then, I've also done some serious thinking about how this life-changing experience also applies to my ministry. Ministry is a wonderful opportunity to serve God. It is exhausting, fulfilling, and rewarding, all at the same time. However, ministry also requires that you constantly look at your heart, because losing your heart for ministry can occur quickly and with devastating consequences. It's easy to rationalize when the warning signs appear.

You may find yourself making excuses to God about how well your ministry is going, just as I did in the face of my doctor's report. Maybe, as I did, you protest that you are immune from such difficulties. During the next five weeks of study, I challenge you to consider the same reminder my physician gave me in the face of my excuses: "It's your life; it's your heart."

Over the next five weeks, you will learn the importance of paying attention to the spiritual condition of your heart and how to detect warning signs that your heart is not where it should be. You will focus on
- how God lovingly and gently watches and judges your heart,
- how your heart holds the ultimate treasure,
- the importance of seeking God with your whole heart, and
- how to minister with a heart like His.

I pray that during the study of *Keeping Your Heart for Ministry,* you will see that without a heart for ministry, all your labors are cold, formal, artificial, and hypocritical. Let your ministry spring from a heart set on fire by God! I pray you will open your heart to a fresh wind of the Holy Spirit, allowing Him to warm your heart with His Word.

Notes

Week 1, Day 1

DISCOVERING A LOST HEART

This Week

One summer when I was about 10 years old, our family set off on a vacation across the New Mexico desert. After stopping for a picnic lunch, we were cheerfully making our way down the highway when suddenly my mother screamed that her purse was missing! She had left her purse at the rest area, now some 30 miles behind us. Not only did the purse contain all the information about our trip, it also contained all of our money. You can imagine the scene that occurred in the car during the next five minutes. We experienced fear, frustration, anger, and much loud talking!

My father turned the car around, and we made our way back to the rest area. Thankfully, the purse was lying just where she had left it — beside the picnic table where we had eaten.

This story illustrates a highly important principle about the heart. Sometimes in the ministry, you are serving the Lord, doing what He has called you to do, when you discover — just as my mother did — that you have lost something of great value along the way. Like that purse, I once discovered that I had lost my heart for ministry.

I can't say specifically that things in my church weren't going well, or that I was in a crisis. I simply had lost the fire, the passion for ministry that once burned in my heart. My work had become mechanical. I was simply going through the motions, doing tasks I had to perform in the course of a day. I attended meetings, prepared sermons, and took care of administrative responsibilities, but I had lost purpose in my work. I felt empty and cold, and my heart was far from the work God had called me to do. This is difficult for me to admit even now. I had been a pastor for more than 20 years. I had always prided myself on my ability to do the work of ministry. I was well-educated, with years of church experience. But something was missing. As with my mother's purse, the only solution for me was to go back, search for my heart, and discover where I had left it.

Before you read further, I want you to consider something. You'll learn more of the warning signs later, but for now, go with what you know. Do you see any warning signs that you might have lost your heart for ministry? If so, list them here.

____
____
____
____
____

What does the Bible mean by the term *heart*? The term refers to something far more than merely a physical organ in the body. The word "heart" in the Bible is used to describe "man's inner nature."[1] The heart expresses all aspects of the inner person — the conscience, the mind, the will, and the emotions.

Characteristics of a "Lost" Heart

Recognizing the fact that you have lost your heart for ministry, or putting it another way, recognizing that your heart is not right with God, is crucial. Scripture lists at least four dangerous conditions of the heart:

1. **The Perverse Heart** — Read the verses in the margin. God is not pleased with the perverse heart. Such a person actually finds joy in perverting the truth and confusing others with untruth.

   One pastor reflected on some of his recent sermon illustrations. While he disliked thinking of himself as guilty of outright lying, he realized that he often managed to exaggerate some of his stories — to make them a little more dramatic or extreme than the actual facts. He rationalized that it was acceptable to take liberties with the facts in order to make a point. But the Holy Spirit prompted him to realize that he was guilty of having a perverse heart. Remember, a perverse heart can cause you to lose your heart for ministry.

The Lord detests men of perverse heart but he delights in those whose ways are blameless.
–Proverbs 11:20

A man of perverse heart does not prosper; he whose tongue is deceitful falls into trouble.
–Proverbs 17:20

Week 1, Day 1

DISCOVERING A LOST HEART *continued . . .*

People in leadership positions sometimes foster gossip or fail to stop it in its tracks. They may refuse to halt confusion by failing to clear the air and stating facts. Leaders frequently become embittered as mean-spirited people seem to prosper. They may not have the courage to sort through a situation so that the truth can be known. Deception, bitterness, or cowardice will eventually rob them of their heart for ministry.

A good test to apply to your heart when you confront a church dispute is to ask, "How am I contributing to a solution?" Don't deceive yourself by thinking you are not part of the problem when you merely repeat what others have said. Unless we actively seek a solution — through prayer, confession, and personal commitment to biblical models for church unity — we remain part of the problem.

Can you think of other ways that someone in ministry can develop a perverse heart? List them here.

____

____

____

There is deceit in the hearts of those who plot evil . . . .
–Proverbs 12:20

2. **The Deceitful Heart** — Read the verse in the margin. The deceitful-hearted person deceives others but also deceives himself or herself.

   When you think of evil in a church setting, you may immediately think about dishonesty, misappropriation of funds, or mean-spirited activities clearly designed to hurt others. But other types of deceit can be just as deadly — more subtle perhaps, but just as harmful.

   What about control issues? Do you know of a pastor, staff member, or committee chairperson who must always have things his or her way? Others may come forward with good proposals, but the leader ignores them — not on their merit but because those ideas don't emanate from the leader himself. Evil springs from these situations just as surely as it does from stealing from the church or from open conflict. This type of spirit can kill the ministry-oriented heart.

3. **The Proud Heart.** Scripture tells us the proud heart is an abomination to God. See the verses in the margin that speak of this type of pride.

How is it possible for a believer to be deceived? Read an excerpt from the startling testimony of Bob Harrington, at one time known as the Chaplain of Bourbon Street.

> I had fame, but when you get famous you start thinking, "Look at what I am doing." After I got saved, I grew too fast — I didn't have a good, stable foundation. It's nobody's fault but mine, but when you get invitations to come give your testimony, you start adding more dates to it. I had to drop out of seminary because I was preaching two revivals a month. I was so caught up in being an evangelist. Money gets to flowing and you find yourself riding in a big customized bus, you find yourself flying in a Lear jet and you find your staff members picking up your briefcases. Unless you've got a solid base, you can really fall into this. I started believing all my cockiness and all my press releases — and that precedes the fall.

Though Bob came to himself some 17 years later and received cleansing and forgiveness from God, he paid a high price for allowing himself to be deceived.

> I'm closer to the Lord than I've ever been . . . . I've learned that I've got to walk daily with the Lord . . . . I want my hearers and readers to know the value of a personal testimony. It's the most valuable possession a human being can have, way above house, home, education, health and family. When you lose your testimony, there's so much more that you've lost.[2]

The Lord detests all the proud of heart. Be sure of this: They will not go unpunished.
–Proverbs 16:5

Before his downfall a man's heart is proud.
–Proverbs 18:12

Haughty eyes and a proud heart, the lamp of the wicked, are sin!
–Proverbs 21:4

Week 1, Day 1

DISCOVERING A LOST HEART *continued . . .*

What are some ways that you have seen a proud heart diminish a person's ministry? Check any descriptions below that apply.

- ❑ An egotistical attitude
- ❑ Failure to listen to others' wise counsel
- ❑ Taking credit for church accomplishments instead of crediting God
- ❑ Failure to confess sin
- ❑ Failure to set an example of humility
- ❑ Other ____

Today, if you hear his voice, do not harden your hearts as you did in the rebellion.
–Hebrews 3:8

But encourage one another daily, as long as it is called Today, so that none of you may be hardened by sin's deceitfulness.
–Hebrews 3:13

Blessed is the man who always fears the Lord, but he who hardens his heart falls into trouble.
–Proverbs 28:14

4. **The Hard Heart.** Read the verses in the margin to see what the Bible says about the hard-hearted person.

   How can a person be "hardened by sin's deceitfulness," as Hebrews 3:13 says? Here's one sad example: In the early part of his ministry, one church official had a sterling reputation for being approachable, personable, and highly interested in people. As the Lord prospered him, he moved to positions of increasing responsibility. However, this leader, once known for his humility, became prideful. He began misappropriating church funds and became blatantly cruel to people. When confronted, he refused to confess his sin. Sin had managed to deceive him about how far he had fallen. His heart had become hardened to the sinful state of his life.

   You (or any leader) are on dangerous ground when you construct barriers to prevent others from confronting you with the truth. We often see a model for this behavior in marriage. A wife refuses to confront her husband's reckless spending, knowing that the price will be sullen silence for weeks. A husband delays telling his wife about a new opportunity in another state, knowing he will face tears and tantrums. A staff member refuses to challenge what he considers an unwise expenditure, knowing he may jeopardize his position.

   The leader who desires to keep his or her heart for ministry will be open to question or challenge, realizing that "iron sharpens iron" (Proverbs 27:17). God graciously provides good counsel to help us continue growing throughout our Christian experience.

Look back at these four traits of a "lost" heart. Stop and pray, asking God to reveal to you whether any of these conditions apply to you. Ask Him to prick your conscience so you can be alert to how this study applies to you specifically.

A Leader Who Lost His Heart for God
The stories of the kings of Israel are good illustrations for leaders today. They demonstrate just how easily *your* heart can be drawn away.

The wisest man who ever lived was King Solomon. God greatly blessed him with wealth and honor. When he came to the throne, he asked God for something very important. His request was for "a discerning heart" (1 Kings 3:9). His request pleased the Lord. As a result, God greatly blessed the reign of Solomon (1 Kings 3:11). Never did a man exist who was his equal. His wisdom, honor, and abilities were known around the world. God blessed him because he sought to have the right kind of heart as he led Israel. But something happened to this wise man. He lost his heart. In fact, he gave his heart away. How could such a thing happen, in light of such an auspicious beginning?

In the verses in the margin, underscore words or phrases that indicate what happened to Solomon.

He had seven hundred wives of royal birth and three hundred concubines, and his wives led him astray. As Solomon grew old, his wives turned his heart after other gods, and his heart was not fully devoted to the Lord his God, as the heart of David his father had been. He followed Ashtoreth the goddess of the Sidonians, and Molech the detestable god of the Ammonites. So Solomon did evil in the eyes of the Lord; he did not follow the Lord completely, as David his father had done.
—1 Kings 11:3-6

At the end of his life, when he should have been the wisest, Solomon ended his reign foolishly — building temples and offering sacrifices to false gods. Despite his great wisdom, he was unable to apply spiritual truth to his own household! The man who said "The fear of the Lord is the beginning of wisdom" allowed idol worship to enter his life. Could such a thing happen to you or to me?

I am reminded of a young man who began his preaching ministry in very humble circumstances. It was clear almost from the start that God would use him in winning many to Christ. Early on, he surrounded himself with trusted advisors — young and old. He purposed in his heart to live a life above reproach so that he could be an effective and bold witness.

Week 1, Day 1

DISCOVERING A LOST HEART *continued . . .*

At a time when it was uncommon, the young man resolved never to be in the company of a woman other than his wife while traveling. Moreover, he made it a practice to have one of his trusted aides go into every hotel room before he entered to make certain there were no other persons there, and so that they could confirm that he stayed alone.

That young man went on to see hundreds of thousands of people around the globe accept Jesus as Savior. Although Billy Graham is known in nearly every corner of the world today, in his eighties he is still that same humble servant.

Above all else, guard your heart, for it is the wellspring of life.
–Proverbs 4:23

Keeping Your Heart for Ministry
The solution to avoiding a lost heart is keeping (guarding) your heart (see Proverbs 4:23, NIV, in the margin) This passage teaches you that you have a spiritual responsibility to keep your heart. The Hebrew text is emphatic. It says "keeping with all, keep" your heart. Set a double guard on your heart. Consider how you would secure a storage building that contained your most valuable possessions. Likely you'd put several locks on it — including a deadbolt, to keep it safe from theft or vandalism.

Keep your heart like a soldier set on the wall of a city under attack by an aggressive enemy. This soldier would look outward to guard against outside attack while also watching to see that the city would not be overthrown from within by traitors among its citizens.

Keep your heart with all diligence, For out of it spring the issues of life.
–Proverbs 4:23

Keeping the heart is a lifelong spiritual responsibility. The verse at left (NKJV) tells you to do it "with all diligence." Regardless of your leadership assignments or your abilities, keep your heart for ministry.

A church staff member was a highly gifted speaker. He was frequently asked to address schools, civic organizations, and even other church groups in the city where he lived. One year his denomination asked him to be one of the preachers at its annual, national meeting — a high honor for him. Sadly, those around him noted a gradual personality change in this leader. He became impressed with his own abilities; he became conceited. He was not the same person he once was. His talents in ministry did not keep his heart from being under attack. The very gifts that enabled him to be effective became an obstacle to ministry. Pride diluted his ability to minister.

Why is keeping your heart so important? Proverbs 4:23 reveals "it is the wellspring of life." Everything comes from the heart. All of your actions flow from the heart. Jesus said, "out of the overflow of the heart the mouth speaks" (Matthew 12:34). Out of the heart flows the passion for ministry. As my physician reminded me, "It's your life; it's your heart!" I would challenge you — "It's *your* heart; it's *your* ministry."

Summary Points to Ponder

- Losing your heart for ministry is possible.
- Your heart can become perverse.
- Your heart can become deceitful.
- Your heart can become proud.
- Your heart can become hard.
- You must diligently keep your heart.

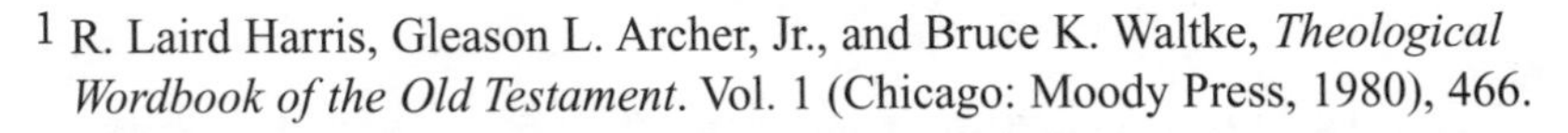

1 R. Laird Harris, Gleason L. Archer, Jr., and Bruce K. Waltke, *Theological Wordbook of the Old Testament*. Vol. 1 (Chicago: Moody Press, 1980), 466.

2 Excerpt from *SBC Life*, November 2000, pages 8-9, published by the SBC Executive Committee. Used by permission.

Notes

Week 1, Day 2

SOMEONE IS WATCHING YOU

This Week

When I was in high school, I dreamed of becoming a Secret Service agent. I was fascinated by the exciting life these agents seem to have. The element of adventure in their work appealed to me. I spent many hours reading and learning about this profession.

As a high school junior, I went to the federal building in my hometown to learn more about the Secret Service. I obtained directions on where to park and how to gain access to this division of the U.S. Department of the Treasury. When I arrived, I got lost. I parked in the wrong parking area. I went to the wrong building. I forgot the names of the agents that I was to meet!

After some time of confusion, I got directions and was back on my way to meet the agents I had come to see. As the elevator doors opened, two men in dark suits greeted me. I told them, with embarrassment, that I had become lost and apologized for being late. They smiled and responded, "That's fine. We've been watching you since you drove into the parking garage!"

A wonderful help in keeping my heart for ministry is recognizing that God is watching my heart! Unlike those agents, God watches my heart because He cares for me and wants only the best for my life and ministry. (See Revelation 2:23 in the margin.) When I consider God's watchfulness over my heart, I am motivated to do my ministry with a pure heart.

Then all the churches will know that I am he who searches hearts and minds, and I will repay each of you according to your deeds.
—Revelation 2:23

God Watches the Motives of Your Heart

Whatever is done for the Lord in ministry must come from pure motives. The Lord watches and searches out the intentions of your heart. David reminded Solomon of this truth. (See 1 Chronicles 28:9 in the margin.) In my prayer time, I ask God to help me examine my intentions and my motivations to make sure they are pure before Him. David said, "Search me, O God, and know my heart; test me and know my anxious thoughts. See if there is any offensive way in me, and lead me in the way everlasting" (Psalm 139:23-24).

And you, my son Solomon, acknowledge the God of your father, and serve him with wholehearted devotion and with a willing mind, for the Lord searches every heart and understands every motive behind the thoughts.
—1 Chronicles 28:9

A woman I know who is regarded as an outstanding Sunday School teacher tells the story of a time when she ministered with impure motives. After moving to a new town from her long-time home, a church leader approached her about teaching young adults. The woman was flattered that her new church so quickly recognized her gifts. Eager to immediately have a role and carve out a niche for herself, she agreed to take the assignment — without even stopping to ask God if He approved. She did the right thing for the wrong reason. Her motives were impure. After only a few months of teaching, the woman resigned her post. God was not honoring her service, her class was not thriving, and she realized she had made a big mistake. She was serving God for her own benefit, not out of obedience to Him. This woman vowed that she would never again take on any assignment without first asking God to examine her heart and her motives.

Can you identify with this story? Have you ever served God with motives that were misdirected or impure? If so, describe here.

____

____

____

____

____

What did you learn from this experience?

____

____

____

____

God Looks at the Heart and not the Outward Appearance

The world judges a person by appearance, performance, and by the actions of his or her life. In much the same way, churches today judge ministry effectiveness by outward appearances — by the number of programs or participants. When Samuel searched for the new king for the nation of Israel, he was told to anoint the red-haired sheepherder as the new king! He must have been shocked when told these words because the Lord reminded Samuel, "The Lord does not look at the things man looks at. Man looks at the outward appearance, but the Lord looks at the heart" (1 Samuel 16:7).

Notes

Week 1, Day 2

SOMEONE IS WATCHING YOU *continued . . .*

Notes

Remembering that God looks at your heart and not the external aspects of your work can be encouraging. Sometimes you may serve in difficult places. In your eyes, the results seem so small and insignificant. However, as He looks at your heart, God knows if you serve with a heart like His. He never regards obedience as small and insignificant.

I am reminded of a story that Pastor Johnny Hunt often shares. He tells of his experience as a very new Christian, when he first felt God's call to preach. He describes himself as quite possibly the world's most unlikely candidate for the ministry. Uneducated, with no Christian background, no job skills — how could he possibly be used, he wondered.

But God moved a Christian layman to step forward when Johnny surrendered to preach, and that layman volunteered to fund his college and seminary education. He was obedient to what God had asked him to do and provided generously and graciously not only for the education expenses, but also for many special gifts for Johnny's wife and children. That layman, now in heaven, could not have known the thousands of people that would be impacted by Johnny's ministry. I suspect he has welcomed many of them, as they entered heaven. God saw potential in Johnny, and in the layman that supported him, that would never have been apparent from outward appearances.

Has God ever moved you to do something you felt totally unqualified to do? If so, describe how you felt, and how you responded.

____
____
____
____

Has God ever moved you to support a person, a task, or a ministry that seemed hopeless to you? Describe your feelings and the outcome of this experience. ____
____
____
____
____

Jot down how your heart condition affected your decision to commit to this ministry. ______________________________________
____
____
____

God is aware if your heart is right and will honor your commitment to Him, even if obvious indicators of success are not present in your work. God knows, and He cares.

O righteous God, who searches minds and hearts, bring to an end the violence of the wicked and make the righteous secure.
–Psalm 7:9

The crucible for silver and the furnace for gold, but the Lord tests the heart.
–Proverbs 17:3

All a man's ways seem right to him, but the Lord weighs the heart.
–Proverbs 21:2

God Tests Your Heart

No one enjoys a test. But one way in which God can see what is truly in your heart is through testing. Read Psalm 7:9 and Proverbs 17:3 at right. Throughout Scripture we have examples of God testing the hearts of his people. A test reveals what you really know and who you are. Trouble in a Christian's life opens up what is in his heart. Like a clerk at the market weighs your produce before you purchase it, God weighs the intentions, motivations, and passion of your heart in ministry. (See Proverbs 21:2 at right.)

Avery Willis, author of *MasterLife*, tells of a test he underwent while waiting to be appointed to the mission field. After resisting a call to missions for many years, Avery finally yielded and surrendered to serve as a missionary overseas. But even then, God did not give him the freedom to go. He served in several U. S. pastorates for about 10 years before the way eventually opened for Avery and his wife, Shirley, to be appointed to Indonesia. He now realizes that the intervening time was God's way of testing his heart and his commitment to the ministry to which he was called.

Have you experienced testing in your ministry? Check any of the following that apply.

- ❑ Personal criticism and/or verbal attack
- ❑ Uncertain results after a major investment of time and effort
- ❑ Physical setbacks, such as personal illness
- ❑ Family difficulties
- ❑ Isolation, loneliness
- ❑ Other ______________________________________

Week 1, Day 2

SOMEONE IS WATCHING YOU *continued . . .*

What do you believe each test revealed about the intentions, motivations, and passions of your heart? ____

____

____

____

Would not God have discovered it, since he knows the secrets of the heart?
–Psalm 44:21

God Will Reveal the Hidden Secrets of Your Heart

The psalmist reminds us that God knows the secrets of the heart. Read the verse in the margin. Although ministry can occur even when you carry secret sins that displease God in your heart, God knows all secrets. Nothing is hidden from Him. He sees your heart and judges whether you are doing your work out of love for Him or out of obligation or guilt. He is aware of those things that you hide from others so successfully. In Psalm 19:12, David said, "who can discern his errors? Forgive my hidden faults."

For we must all appear before the judgment seat of Christ, that each one may receive what is due him for the things done while in the body, whether good or bad.
–2 Corinthians 5:10

Therefore judge nothing before the appointed time; wait till the Lord comes. He will bring to light what is hidden in darkness and will expose the motives of men's hearts. At that time each will receive his praise from God.
–1 Corinthians 4:5

When you stand before the judgement seat of Christ, He promises to reveal the hidden secrets of your heart. Read the last two passages at left. On that day, the secrets that you've told no other person will be revealed. The suffering that you have borne, the difficulties you have endured in secret, the pain you have experienced in ministry will be revealed. Each person will receive praise for bearing those burdens for the cause of Christ.

But perhaps, as you read these words, your heart also convicts you of secret sins like David. Can you name those secret sins? Perhaps one is pride — you may have been too proud to listen to other people or too proud to humble yourself before the Lord and seek His direction for the church you pastor or for the committee you chair. Perhaps you've insisted on doing things your way instead of seeking others' godly counsel. Your ego may get in your way — you delight in the sound of your own voice and forget that you are but God's mouthpiece as you preach, teach, or lead. Perhaps your ministry is taking more and more of your time and you are finding so much identity in it that you no longer delight in the company of your family. Perhaps your secret sin is a "works" mentality. It is tempting to think achievements and accomplishments will make you seem more worthy in God's eyes, or that work will even cover up some past wrongdoing in your life.

Notes

As you keep your heart in ministry, confess your secret sins to God. Your heart cannot be set on fire in a fresh, new way if sin prevents you from having a pure heart before Him. Today, pause and remember that God watches your heart.

In the paragraphs that you just read, can you identify with any of these secret sins? If so underline one or more. If none of yours are listed specifically, try to focus on one that applies to you. Stop and confess it to God, asking Him to give you the courage to set things right so that your heart can be pure again. Ask the Holy Spirit to help you keep your heart pure.

Summary Points to Ponder

- The Lord Jesus searches your mind and heart.
- God doesn't look at outward appearances but on the heart.
- God examines your intentions and motives in ministry.
- God tests your intentions so you can see your own heart.
- At the Second Coming, God will openly reveal the secrets of your heart.
- Healing, restoration, and forgiveness are yours for the asking!

Week 1, Day 3

FINDING REAL TREASURE IN YOUR HEART

This Week

A friend of mine loves to hunt. He reads about hunting, watches television about hunting, and surfs the Internet about hunting. Each year he goes on hunting trips to some of the world's most exotic places. His trips cost thousands of dollars. He spends enormous amounts of money on equipment to make sure that he is able to bag his prey. When you visit his home, you know that you are in the presence of an accomplished hunter. As you walk into his den, you see stuffed trophies of some of his hunting expeditions. If you blink too quickly, you might think that these animals are still alive. He calls these stuffed animals his "treasures." The fact that my friend puts his whole heart into his hunting is very clear.

Where Is Your Treasure?
You can apply the same principle to your life. Whatever you put your heart into reveals what you treasure. Jesus reminded His disciples of this important principle in the Sermon on the Mount. In Matthew 6:21 He said, "Where your treasure is, there your heart will be also."

God is to be our first priority; a relationship with Him must top our list of treasures. Our second priority is to be our family. Many leaders who say they treasure their families spend so little time with them that family members feel anything but "treasured." A pastor friend often says, "We practice that which we believe. Everything else is religious talk." If you treasure your relationship with God, finding time for Him will take precedence over all that competes for your time. Likewise, if you treasure your family, spending time with them will become a priority.

Spotting what you treasure is easy. When you treasure someone, you spend time thinking about that person. You protect the things you treasure. When you treasure something, you are willing to make great sacrifices for it. No cost is too great for the things or the people you treasure.

So, what do you treasure? Take a few minutes and consider how you would respond to the following questions. Then write your answers.

What kinds of things occupy your mind?

____

____

For whom or what are you willing to sacrifice?

____

____

What things or people do you value above everything else?

____

____

As you answer these questions, you find your treasure — and there you find your heart.

Treasures in Heaven

In this same sermon, Jesus challenges His disciples, "Do not store up for yourselves treasures on earth . . . but store up for yourselves treasures in heaven . . ." (Matthew 6:19-20). You may find that you use the majority of your time storing up treasures here on earth. So much of your life is spent saving, sacrificing, struggling, and worrying about your earthly treasures. Sadly, these someday will belong to someone else! See the passage in the margin.

But God said to him, "You fool! This very night your life will be demanded from you. Then who will get what you have prepared for yourself?"
–Luke 12:20

The challenge then, is to set your heart on eternal treasures, and store them up. Your ministry is a wonderful treasure God has given you! A ministry for God is a way to store up treasures in heaven. While you don't always clearly understand your impact on others' eternal destiny, some day in heaven you will see the fruit of your labors.

A well-to-do woman in southern Illinois was just such a person. Mrs. Cross lived a very simple lifestyle. Her tiny cottage at the edge of town certainly gave no appearance of wealth. Her habit was to be the first to volunteer when help was needed. She could always be counted on to entertain the church staff and visiting ministers. Secretly, and without fanfare, she supported several families in the community who were having trouble making

Week 1, Day 3

FINDING REAL TREASURE IN YOUR HEART *continued . . .*

Notes

ends meet. She could have chosen otherwise. She could have had a nicer home, driven a bigger car, and spent more on clothes. But she had other priorities; her focus was on heaven.

Go back to the next to last paragraph you just read. Underline the statement, "Your ministry is a wonderful treasure God has given you!" Is this how you feel about your ministry? Stop and pray, asking God to search your heart and help you remember what a precious gift your ministry is to you.

The New Testament figure Epaphroditus was a man who found his treasure in his ministry. He was sick and almost died, yet he was eager to minister to the church at Philippi. Paul says about Epaphroditus, "he almost died for the work of Christ, risking his life to make up for the help you could not give me" (Philippians 2:30).

Here is an example of a man who stored up treasure in heaven. No cost was too great, no thought of personal comfort was on his mind. He had in his heart the burning desire to minister to God's people. His ministry was his treasure!

What would keep missionaries Joyce and David Harms on the field in Honduras for more than 30 years? At a time when many of their age have opted for the comforts of home and family, these two committed people have continued their labor of love in Honduras. Years of godly living and service have won them the respect of the saved and unsaved, those of humble status, and those at the highest levels of government. Their love for the Lord and the people of that needy country is their treasure.

Have you ever asked God to reprioritize your earthly treasures in order to put your heart more into the work of the Kingdom? If so, describe here.

Today, ask God to show you your treasure. Pause and reflect on the things in which you invest your time. Would God consider them earthly or heavenly treasures? Ask God to help you get a fresh vision of how you can lay up treasures in heaven.

Summary Points to Ponder

- Wherever your treasure is, you will find your heart there.
- Heavenly treasures are eternal; earthly treasures are temporary.
- Your ministry is an eternal treasure from God.
- To keep your heart for ministry requires you to regularly assess your treasures.

Notes

Week 1, Day 4

SEEKING GOD WITH YOUR WHOLE HEART

This Week

I have always prided myself in being a hard-working person. From my earliest years in high school throughout college, I worked at different kinds of jobs. I was a janitor, a retail clerk, a paper carrier, and a gas-station attendant. None of these jobs were glamorous, but they met my financial needs. Perhaps more importantly, they represented opportunities for me to learn responsibility and discipline.

I did have one other job that I didn't mention. While I was in seminary, I worked for two days on a cement crew. Notice I said I worked for only two days because, well, I was fired! That's right — fired from a cement crew. It was in Fort Worth, Texas; it was summertime, and it was hot. I was soft; I really didn't want to be out there. I had no real commitment to the job. After the second day, the foreman came to me and said, "Mike, I'm sorry, but I'll have to let you go." In shock, I asked, "Why?" He replied, "Because when you do concrete work, you have to do it with all your heart. It's obvious you aren't putting your heart into it."

The interesting thing about that experience was that I knew my heart wasn't in the work, but I didn't realize the foreman could see it, too. I suspect there are coworkers, family members, or friends who know when *your* heart is not in your work. They can see when your ministry suffers. But ministry for God requires that you put your heart into it — your whole heart.

Blessings Occur When You Seek God Wholeheartedly

Consider the well-known testimony of a man who had a heart for God. King David wrote a masterful psalm – Psalm 119 – under the Holy Spirit's inspiration. In this wonderful passage, he uses each letter of the Hebrew alphabet to speak of the wonder and power of the Word of God. He gives glimpses into his own walk with God. His language expresses for believers of all generations the power of seeking God with a whole heart.

Read the three verses in the left and top right margins. In each, underline words or phrases stating what will happen when someone seeks God with a whole heart.

Blessed are they who keep his statutes and seek him with all their heart. –*Psalm 119:2*

So if you faithfully obey the commands I am giving you today–to love the Lord your God and to serve him with all your heart and with all your soul–then I will send rain on your land in its season, both autumn and spring rains, so that you may gather in your grain, new wine and oil. –*Deuteronomy 11:13*

(Continued in next column . . .)

These verses testify that God's blessing comes when people obey the Word of God and seek Him with a whole heart. Some of us, however, are like Amaziah the king, who did what was right in the sight of the Lord "but not wholeheartedly" (2 Chronicles 25:2).

In everything he undertook in the service of God's temple and in obedience to the law and the commands, he sought his God and worked wholeheartedly. And so he prospered.
—2 Chronicles 31:21

How does a lack of heart manifest itself in ministry? Perhaps you're somewhat like I was on the cement crew job — showing up for work, but with a lackadaisical attitude, just going through the motions but without any fervor behind it. Perhaps you're still teaching a Sunday School class but with only minimal preparation, just enough to get by, but without the serious study, prayer, and outreach that makes a difference. Perhaps you are putting in your prescribed time in your church's prayer ministry, but while you are supposed to be praying for those on the prayer list, your mind wanders to your own needs and interests. When this happens, your heart probably isn't truly in your task.

Obey with Your Whole Heart

Your heart is revealed in your willingness to obey God. You must have an active, determined desire in your heart to obey God at all costs. David prayed, "Give me understanding, and I will keep your law and obey it with all my heart" (Psalm 119:34). As you read and study God's Word, you gain understanding into His will for you. As you understand God's Word, you can obey from the heart, as David did. Read 1 Kings 14:8 in the margin.

I tore the kingdom away from the house of David and gave it to you, but you have not been like my servant David, who kept my commands and followed me with all his heart, doing only what was right in my eyes.
—1 Kings 14:8

Describe an experience when your study of God's Word gave you understanding that helped you obey with your whole heart. *(Example: I wanted to quit when I heard some criticism of my church committee's project. I read in 2 Chronicles 20:1-30 about allowing God to fight my battles. I believe this passage encouraged me to persevere despite obstacles.)*

____

____

____

____

____

____

Week 1, Day 4

SEEKING GOD WITH YOUR WHOLE HEART *continued . . .*

Notes

Pray with Your Whole Heart

Seeking God with a whole heart includes praying with your whole heart — not holding back, being distracted by outside thoughts, but completely seeking God in prayer. David said, "I have sought your face with all my heart . . . . I call with all my heart; answer me, O Lord" (Psalm 119:58,145). I know several leaders who deliberately set aside a half day monthly for concentrated prayer and spending time with the Master, so they can focus without interruption on what God has to say to them and what they say in response to God. Even if you can't work a regular extended prayer time like this into your schedule, try to determine ways you can work more wholehearted, committed, undistracted prayer into your life.

Some ways I have done (or will try to do) this are:

- Turn off the television or wrap up other activities earlier at night to make room for prayer time before I go to bed;
- Set my alarm a half-hour earlier each morning to devote time to prayer and God's Word;
- Take my Bible and prayer materials with me to work and pray during my lunch hour, with the door to my office closed;
- Keep a prayer journal to record prayer requests and answers;
- Keep a list of unsaved persons and other specific needs to pray for on a regular basis;
- Other ____

Prayer will help you keep your heart for ministry. As you persist in prayer, you discover what God wants you to do. Heart work is done in prayer. Keeping your heart in ministry occurs as you seek God with your whole heart.

Pause to pray right now. Ask God to draw you to regular conversation with Him in prayer. Ask Him to give you the discipline, creativity, and motivation to commune with Him on a regular basis and to seek Him with a whole heart.

Summary Points to Ponder

- God blesses those who seek Him with a whole heart.
- Ministry deserves wholehearted effort.
- God blesses wholehearted ministry.
- Wholehearted prayer is essential to ministry.

Notes

Week 1, Day 5

MINISTRY WITH A HEART LIKE GOD'S

This Week

The first time I served on a church staff, I was a 17-year-old youth minister just starting college. I was fortunate to work on the staff of a wonderful pastor who had served faithfully for many years.

As a young minister I had no idea what ministry was all about. I was unsure of myself and was overwhelmed by the great needs I saw throughout the church. But Pastor Harvey was willing to take me under his guidance and help me learn how to do my job.

In the years I served with Pastor Harvey, I never heard him utter a critical word about individuals or the church as a whole. I often walked by his office at different times of the day and heard him praying. With strong cries and tears, he lifted the church's needs to the Lord. As I listened, I felt I had stumbled onto a private conversation between my pastor and the Lord.

But perhaps the greatest memory I have of Pastor Harvey was how he ministered from his heart. Often I stood with him at a graveside as he wept with family members in their loss. He took me along as he visited hospitals and elder-care centers. He served the people under his care with a heart like God's. I not only learned from and observed his ministry from the heart, I saw results in the lives of the people in the church and the community. Pastor Harvey was loved and respected because of his heart for the ministry. He often advised me, "Mike, don't be afraid to let people see your heart."

Do you know someone like Pastor Harvey? Perhaps you've had a pastor, a staff member, a coworker, or a lay leader who was instrumental in your life and who demonstrated God's heart in the ministry. If so, describe that person here.

____

____

____

____

I stated that I saw in the lives of people around him the results of Pastor Harvey's "heart ministry." Can you see the result of your ministering from the heart in the life of someone in your church or your community?

Describe that situation here.

____
____
____
____
____
____

Having a Heart Like God

When Israel was far from God, Jeremiah the prophet called the people to repentance. He promised God's forgiveness and blessing on the nation if the people would return to God. He promised to give Israel shepherds after His heart. Read Jeremiah 3:15 in the margin.

Then I will give you shepherds after my own heart, who will lead you with knowledge and understanding.
– Jeremiah 3:15

Today as you think about your ministry, ask yourself this question: Am I conducting my ministry with a heart like God? Am I a shepherd after His heart?

Ministers with a heart like God are compassionate and sensitive to the needs of those to whom they minister. The gospel writers tell us on more than one occasion, that Jesus showed compassion for the people. One of those Scriptures is Matthew 9:36, appearing in the margin.

When he saw the crowds, he had compassion on them, because they were harassed and helpless, like sheep without a shepherd.
–Matthew 9:36

God has placed you in your ministry and calls you to do your work with a heart like His. Keeping your heart in ministry requires a heart like God's. Jeremiah was broken-hearted because the prophets and priests of his day demonstrated a lack of heart in their ministry. He said, "Concerning the prophets; My heart is broken within me; all my bones tremble . . . . both prophet and priest are godless" (Jeremiah 23:9, 11). As a result of their sin, the land was full of ungodliness (Jeremiah 23:15).

Recall the last time your heart was broken for the people you serve. Perhaps it was broken for your congregation. Your heart may be broken for an unsaved person to whom you are ministering. Describe the last

Week 1, Day 5

MINISTRY WITH A HEART LIKE GOD'S

continued . . .

time you can honestly say you were heartbroken because of the spiritual condition of others.

I spoke with a member of a church that is in real trouble. The members are sharply divided, some supporting, some vilifying the young pastor. My friend grieves over the unwillingness of this church family — the body of Christ — to come together in prayer and confession to solve this problem. She has quietly approached many who hold leadership roles, seeking reconciliation and forgiveness, apparently to no avail. She confessed that her own heart is utterly broken and that she struggles daily to leave the matter in God's hands. Her broken heart is comforted only in knowing that the church is His. It is, after all, His work, His church, and His pastor.

God's heart is full of compassion and love for the sheep of His pasture. If you minister with His heart, you will have that brokenness of heart that will propel you to serve Him wholeheartedly and not just by rote.

Do not listen to what the prophets are prophesying to you; they fill you with false hopes. They speak visions from their own minds, not from the mouth of the Lord. They keep saying to those who despise me, "The Lord says; You will have peace." And to all who follow the stubbornness of their hearts, they say, "No harm will come to you."
–Jeremiah 23:16-17

Ministry with a Heart Like God's

Read Jeremiah 23:16-17 in the margin. What did the prophets of Jeremiah's day do that displeased the Lord?

The prophets mentioned in these verses spoke from their own hearts, rather than speaking a word from the Lord. They also failed to confront the people about their sin and failed to communicate about God's punishment for their wrongdoing. This contrasts sharply to the directive you read earlier in Jeremiah 3:15, in which shepherds were to feed the people with knowledge and understanding.

Out of a heart that grows in Christlikeness comes a heart for the people to whom you minister. As you hear from God and then speak the truth in love, you demonstrate your heart for God's people. As a result, you minister not for personal recognition or reward but to faithfully carry out your God-given ministry for God's glory. God's people can clearly see when you minister with a heart like His.

Stop and pray, asking the Lord to search your heart and reveal to you whether you are guilty of any of the same things as the prophets of Jeremiah's day. If God reveals to you that you are speaking your own words rather than His or that you are failing to honestly confront those you serve, confess it now. Ask God to cleanse you, and invite His Holy Spirit to help you minister with a heart like His.

Summary Points to Ponder

- God promises to provide His people with ministers who have a heart like His.
- Ministry that pleases God comes from ministers with a heart like God's.
- Ministry lacking a heart like God's does not please the Lord.
- Ministry with a heart like God's feeds the people of God with knowledge and understanding.

Notes

Week 2, Introduction

KEEPING YOUR HEART FOR GOD

This Week

- Day 1: Knowing God – The Relationship of the Heart
- Day 2: Seeking God – The Activity of the Heart
- Day 3: Trusting God – The Security of the Heart
- Day 4: Pleasing God – The Ambition of the Heart
- Day 5: Following God – The Response of the Heart

Another event made a lasting impression on me early in my ministry. I read the books of a minister named Leonard Ravenhill, and his writings on revival and personal holiness stirred my heart. I wrote Rev. Ravenhill and asked to visit him at his home. He agreed, so several friends joined me as I went to talk with this respected minister and author.

During that visit, we spoke of many things — the ministry, the Bible, prayer, and living to please God. But two things he said to us that summer afternoon have stayed with me to this day. First, he said, "Boys, make it your ambition to know God and to please Him before anything else in your life." He then took us to a small closet and opened the door. The closet was covered from ceiling to floor with mirrors. In the center was a kneeling bench and a small table with an open Bible. As we looked inside, Mr. Ravenhill said, "This is the place you must start if you are to know and please Him — knowing God starts in your heart."

Knowing and pleasing God is a heart issue. As you learned in your Week-1 study, keeping your heart is a personal responsibility. To *know* God reminds you that your Lord desires to have a living, powerful relationship with you — and that knowing Him is attainable. Pleasing God expresses your heart's desire to be assured that God is pleased with you.

Perhaps a godly person has challenged you to seek God with all your heart, as Mr. Ravenhill challenged me. Nothing can replace a passion for knowing and pleasing God! That passion must be your first and most important life priority. For God to give you a heart like His, you must desire to be like Him in all your ways.

Keeping your heart for ministry is founded on the principles you will study this week. These days of study will present wonderful opportunities to evaluate your heart relationship with God. This week you will discover the secret to keeping your heart in ministry — a strong and growing walk with God. Ask God to help you examine your heart objectively and honestly. Reflect on your heart condition as you pray and study His Word.

Week 2, Day 1

KNOWING GOD – THE RELATIONSHIP OF THE HEART

Notes

A woman once sat in my office describing her struggle as she tried her best to reconcile with her husband. As their pastor, I had met and prayed repeatedly with them about their marriage. The wife questioned why her husband would not commit himself to make the marriage work. She was hurt and broken by his lack of desire to build a strong and growing relationship with her. She had made numerous attempts to strengthen the relationship, but her husband had rejected her each time. Finally, as she sat in the church office weeping, she lamented, "I have been married to my husband for 25 years, but he has never let me know him!"

How tragic that two people could be married for 25 years, yet not know each other. Is it possible that you have experienced God's saving grace, yet you cannot say you *really know* Him?

Knowing Others and Relationships

Knowing *about* another person is the foundation of a relationship with a neighbor, a friend, a family member, a fellow church member, someone you are dating, or your spouse. Understanding how this person reacts to crisis and trouble, and learning what makes him or her happy and unhappy, is fundamental in all kinds of relationships. The longer you relate to another person, the more you understand that person's ways, interests, needs, and desires. As a relationship grows, you learn how you can best relate to the individual and his or her style of operating.

These same principles are true in your relationship with God. Knowing God is vital if you are to keep your heart in ministry. When David challenged Solomon with his new responsibilities as King of Israel, he reminded Solomon to "acknowledge the God of your father, and serve him with wholehearted devotion and with a willing mind" (1 Chronicles 28:9).

David's words to his son are good advice for you today. You can know God and understand His ways, His desires, and His purposes. Knowing God is a heart matter. David reminded Solomon to know God with "wholehearted devotion" — a heart committed to God and His will.

Week 2, Day 1

KNOWING GOD – THE RELATIONSHIP OF THE HEART *continued . . .*

Think of a time in your life when you served God with wholehearted devotion. As you think about this time, what characterized this period of wholehearted devotion — a heart that was totally set on God and His will? Check any of the statements below that apply.

- ❑ I was especially diligent in having regular quiet times of conversation with God.
- ❑ I demonstrated a servant heart, without need for praise or affirmation for my service.
- ❑ My relationships with others exemplified a Christlike love for them.
- ❑ I sought to eliminate all activities from my life that would interfere with knowing and serving Christ.
- ❑ I prayed, seeking God's will instead of mine.
- ❑ Other ____

If you responded with a type of wholeheartedly devoted relationship that is in the *past* tense, what do you think would be necessary for you to be in this type of relationship again? Describe here.

____

____

____

____

O Lord, you have searched me and you know me. You know when I sit and when I rise.
–Psalm 139:1-2

Then all the churches will know that I am he who searches hearts and minds, and I will repay each of you according to your deeds.
–Revelation 2:23

God Knows You

Establish the ambition of your heart to know God in His ways, His works, and His will. Invest time specifically in getting to know Him intimately and personally. As you come to know Him in these ways, your heart and your ministry will be strengthened.

Remember, the Lord knows your heart. Because you are in relationship with Him, He looks deep within your heart seeking to know you. Scripture reveals that the Lord searches each heart and He tests it. The Scripture passages in the margin remind you that you are in a heart relationship with God.

When your heart is set on knowing God, you will have a heart ready for ministry. As you grow in your knowledge of the Lord, strive to regularly say with the psalmist, "Search me, O God, and know my heart; test me and know my anxious thoughts" (Psalm 139:23).

Stop right now and ask God to search and know your heart, just as the Psalm you just read mentioned. When He searches your heart, what will He find? Will He find a heart that is totally devoted to Him? If so, ask Him to help you keep your heart for Him. If He finds that your heart is less than totally sold out to Him, ask Him to point you back to the right path so that you can know Him more intimately.

Summary Points to Ponder

- Personal knowledge about another person is the basis of a growing relationship.
- To have a growing relationship with God, you must first set your heart on knowing Him.
- When you determine to know God, your heart is prepared for ministry.
- God knows your heart; He understands your ways and tests your heart.
- A heart that knows God is ready for ministry.

Notes

Week 2, Day 2

SEEKING GOD – THE ACTIVITY OF THE HEART

This Week

Day 1: Knowing God – The Relationship of the Heart
Day 2: Seeking God – The Activity of the Heart
Day 3: Trusting God – The Security of the Heart
Day 4: Pleasing God – The Ambition of the Heart
Day 5: Following God – The Response of the Heart

I sought the Lord, and he answered me; he delivered me from all my fears.

–Psalm 34:4

Blessed are they who keep his statues and seek him with all their heart.

–Psalm 119:2

Nothing is as exciting as discovering hidden treasure! When I was 12 years old my family traveled to Colorado, and I went hunting for rubies. I will never forget riding to a spot on the side of a mountain and taking up my hammer and gloves to begin my expedition. I spent all afternoon breaking open rocks searching for those stones! After a while, my hands began to hurt because of the force of the hammer hitting the rocks. But the thought of finding rubies kept me at my task. I was consumed by the hunt.

I didn't find many rubies on that vacation, but I learned a valuable lesson from the experience. I put my whole heart into looking for those stones because I prized them. When you search for something of great value, you put your whole heart into it. In a similar manner, you can seek God.

If my heart is to be ready for ministry, I must make it my life's activity to seek God. I can't recommend that others seek God or inspire them to do so if I'm not modeling this myself. Nothing in life compares with the value of knowing God. Just as I searched for rubies in the rocks of Colorado, I must search for God. That is the activity of my heart. See the verses appearing in the margin. The tools we use in this activity are personal worship, quiet time, His Word, prayer, and reflection.

In Psalm 34:4 at left, underline the phrase that tells what happened when David sought God. In Psalm 119:2, underline the word that tells what happens to individuals when they seek the Lord. What does this word (blessed) mean to you today? ______________________

____

____

David, described as a man after God's own heart, sought the Lord at all times — not just when he felt like it. Could this be said of you, as well?

Do you seek the Lord at all times? ❑ Yes ❑ No
If you answered no, what keeps you from seeking Him?

____

____

A story is told about Martin Luther, the great church reformer. He was confronted one day by his assistant concerning Luther's busy schedule for the hours that lay ahead. Luther replied that he would first start the day in prayer. The assistant was concerned that Luther might not be able to finish all the pressing duties he faced if Luther spent too much time praying. Luther responded, "I have so many things to do today that I must pray for four hours!" Nothing can replace your time of seeking God. It warms your heart and prepares you for your work and ministry. Are you, like Luther, taking the time to seek God?

Psalm 119:2 promises that you will be blessed when you seek the Lord. Jesus promises in Matthew 7:7 at right that if you seek God, you will find him. How do you feel about these promises?

- ❑ I'd like to believe that God is "findable" if I seek Him, but I'm not sure about this. I've never been able to experience Him in the way you've described.
- ❑ I believe that God is "findable," but I feel unworthy. I'm not a good enough Christian. Why would God want to relate to me?
- ❑ I genuinely try to seek God and feel that I do find Him some of the time, but at other times, He seems terribly remote.
- ❑ I seek God and find Him whenever I call on His name. If He seems remote, I know it's because I moved away from Him.
- ❑ Other ____

  ____

  ____

Ask, and it will be given to you; seek and you will find; knock and the door will be opened to you.

–Matthew 7:7

A Person Who Sought God

King Jehoshaphat illustrates how you can seek God. The Bible says of this king, "And the Lord was with Jehoshaphat because in his early years he walked in the ways his father David had followed. He did not consult the Baals but sought the God of his father and followed his commands rather than the practices of Israel" (2 Chronicles 17:3-4). Because of his power, the king could have sought anything. But he chose to seek God. As Scripture records his life and work, it speaks of Jehoshaphat seeking God.

Week 2, Day 2

SEEKING GOD – THE ACTIVITY OF THE HEART *continued . . .*

His heart was devoted to the ways of the Lord; furthermore, he removed the high places and the Asherah poles from Judah.
–2 Chronicles 17:6

Are you thought of as a leader who seeks God? Do those you serve and minister to see you as a man or woman who seeks God? ❑ Yes ❑ No

Read 2 Chronicles 17:6 at left. Underline what his wholehearted devotion to God caused Jehoshaphat to do.

The activity of seeking God characterized Jehoshaphat's life and moved him to action. Because of this singular focus of his life, he turned away from the idolatry of the former kings of Judah. And so it will be with you. When you truly seek Him, you will be moved to do as He directs, and others will be influenced.

Would people recognize you as someone who seeks God with your whole heart? What does this type of devotion lead you to do? Check all statements below that apply.

- ❑ Have a servant heart in my relationships with others
- ❑ Take a godly but unpopular stand on an issue, even if it risked my standing in certain circles
- ❑ Pray fervently for others' needs
- ❑ Speak an encouraging word to someone who is struggling
- ❑ Tell lost persons about Jesus
- ❑ Other ____
  ____

They buried him, for they said, "He was a son of Jehoshaphat, who sought the Lord with all his heart."
–2 Chronicles 22:9

Jehoshaphat became so well known for seeking God that others, years later, described him as the king who sought God with his whole heart. See 2 Chronicles 22:9 at left. Is this the type of legacy that will live after you?

There is, however, some good in you, for you have rid the land of the Asherah poles and have set your heart on seeking God.
–2 Chronicles 19:3

Jehoshaphat was not perfect in all his actions. During his reign, a godly prophet met Jehoshaphat and rebuked him for his alliance with Ahab the king of Israel, yet the prophet commended him for his heart that sought God. (See 2 Chronicles 19:3 at left.) He still failed God on some matters, as you and I will do, but his heart was right with God. When the Bible describes the life and contribution of Jehoshaphat, it says, "He walked in the ways of his father Asa and did not stray from them; he did what was right in the eyes of the Lord" (2 Chronicles 20:32).

Jehoshaphat was not alone in his desire to seek God. The Bible says of Hezekiah, "In everything that he undertook in the service of God's temple and in obedience in the law and the commands, he sought his God and worked wholeheartedly. And so he prospered" (2 Chronicles 31:21).

Seeking God is the activity of the heart. As you seek Him, he blesses you.

Can you think of a time in your life when this has been true of you — when you experienced God's blessing as a result of seeking Him? If so, describe here.

____

____

____

____

In prayer, thank God for the time you just described. If you were unable to focus on a time when this was true, ask God to help you seek Him now so He can pour out His blessings on you.

Summary Points to Ponder

- Make seeking God a priority in your life.
- God blesses those who seek Him.
- Seeking God is the activity of the heart.
- Be known as a leader who seeks God.
- Model seeking God for those you lead.

Notes

Week 2, Day 3

TRUSTING GOD – THE SECURITY OF THE HEART

This Week

Day 1: Knowing God – The Relationship of the Heart
Day 2: Seeking God – The Activity of the Heart
Day 3: Trusting God – The Security of the Heart
Day 4: Pleasing God – The Ambition of the Heart
Day 5: Following God – The Response of the Heart

A conversation that my wife once had with a relative exemplifies the "language of trust" more than just about any statement I ever heard. Immediately after graduation, I felt God leading my family to move to California so I could pastor a church there. California was a long way from Oklahoma, where my wife and I were reared. Nevertheless, our families gave us their blessing.

As we visited our loved ones before we loaded up and headed west to California, a family member commented to my wife, "Pat, you seem so calm and relaxed about this move. Aren't you afraid?" Pat's answer was wonderful. She replied, "I'm not sure what we will face when we get to California, but one thing I am confident about is that God will take care of us!"

The many years we served in California demonstrated the truth of her statement of trust again and again. God took care of us. He always has, and He always will. Trust brings security to the heart. When you don't understand or know where to turn, trust in Him secures your heart.

Loss of Hope, Loss of Heart
To keep your heart for ministry, maintain your trust in God. Nothing destroys your faith any faster than does a loss of hope. The Bible says, "Hope deferred makes the heart sick, but a longing fulfilled is a tree of life" (Proverbs 13:12). Spiritual heart sickness occurs when you lose your trust in God. When your trust is gone, your hope fades away.

Do not let your hearts be troubled. Trust in God; trust also in me.
–John 14:1

Many times in my life, I have struggled with the loss of hope. This still happens to me on occasion. However, when it does, I remember that ministry cannot be done effectively when a person loses trust in God. The same God who called me to ministry is the same God who will help me in times of trouble. The same applies to you today, wherever or however you are serving Him. When Jesus was about to leave the disciples in the upper room, He reminded them not to lose their trust. See John 14:1 in the margin.

Read the following case studies of individuals who lost hope in their ministry. (The characters are fictitious, but their stories represent troublesome situations that can occur in church life.) Below each vignette,

describe one action you believe the person could take if he or she remembered the truth of the verse you just read in John 14:1.

Carl took a job as a youth minister immediately on his graduation from seminary. He quickly bonded with the teenagers in the youth group and began making significant contributions to their lives. However, some of his new programs were instantly opposed by several long-time youth workers, who disliked change. This small but influential group of workers persuaded the pastor to ask for Carl's resignation. Carl became discouraged and began doubting his call to youth ministry.

____

____

____

Judy was the chairman of the church missions committee. She had participated in a life-changing volunteer trip to Venezuela and wanted the church to send a group back to Venezuela the following summer. A member of her committee had relatives in Kenya and wanted Kenya to be the next mission trip site, but other members did not think such a faraway trip was possible for a few years. Hurt feelings resulted, and the member who favored Kenya as a site began spreading untrue gossip about Judy. Judy was disheartened and went to the pastor to resign as chairman of the committee.

____

____

____

Cliff taught eighth-grade boys in Sunday School. Although he had taught for many years, this year's group of boys seemed unresponsive to his teaching methods. Many disrupted the class sessions, and no one seemed willing to share or discuss the week's lesson subject. Cliff stopped his regular visits and phone calls to them because he felt the boys did not relate to him well. He began spending less and less time preparing for his class and used the time he normally would spend on class activities for personal pleasure.

____

____

____

Notes

Week 2, Day 3

TRUSTING GOD – THE SECURITY OF THE HEART *continued . . .*

Now, describe a time in your life when you've experienced a loss of hope in your ministry (perhaps one like Carl, Judy, or Cliff experienced, or something totally different.) How did you get through this time? What, if anything, reassured you? ______________________________

____

____

Trust in the Lord

Keep Jesus Christ as the focus of your trust. You cannot trust in people, in your skills, or in resources, because these are finite and inevitably will fail. Focus your confidence completely on the Lord Jesus Christ. He alone can secure a troubled heart.

For it is with your heart that you believe and are justified, and it is with your mouth that you confess and are saved.
–Romans 10:10

So then, just as you received Christ Jesus as Lord, continue to live in him, rooted and built up in him, strengthened in the faith as you were taught, and overflowing with thankfulness. See to it that no one takes you captive through hollow and deceptive philosophy, which depends on human tradition and the basic principles of this world rather than on Christ.
–Colossians 2:6-8

The Bible calls on you to trust the Lord with all your heart. Proverbs 3:5-6 says, "Trust in the Lord with all your heart and lean not on your own understanding; in all your ways acknowledge him, and he will make your paths straight."

What a wonderful passage for keeping your heart in ministry! You begin the Christian life by faith in Christ. See Romans 10:10 in the margin. You *continue* the Christian life by faith in Christ. See Colossians 2:6-8 in the margin. You cannot live the Christian life without trust in God. You cannot trust Him partially; trust Him wholeheartedly!

This principle would be ideal for the characters in the above case studies to remember as they deal with their situations. Although Carl's situation was painful, it did not have to represent the end of his career in ministry. As he searched his heart and reaffirmed God's call to work with youth, he could trust God to direct him to people — perhaps his seminary professors or other colleagues — who could guide him as he considers God's plans for his future. Perhaps career counseling could help him determine how to deal with church conflicts in the future.

Judy could consult with her pastor or other church staff members about how to deal with the angry committee member. If she continued to feel led to resign, she could trust God to show her how she could continue to wholeheartedly support and encourage missions in her church.

Cliff could examine his own heart, asking God to show him whether his initial difficulties with the class members reflected his own lost heart for ministry. He could seek the counsel of other experienced teachers about how to work with the misbehavior and possibly spend individual time with some of the boys. He could ask God whether he should seek reassignment to another age group or use his gifts in some other area of church service. In all three situations, the individuals could trust God to show them their next step.

Sometimes I try to figure out what God is doing or why He allows certain things to happen in my life and ministry. But in the end, if I want to keep my heart, I must be willing to trust Him with all my heart and not rely on my own understanding.

Assuring Your Heart

When you trust the Lord, a calm assurance arises that neither the world nor current circumstances can take away. Note the verses in the margin. Hebrews 10:22 admonishes you to "draw near to God with a sincere heart in full assurance of faith." When I trust the Lord with my ministry and my heart, I can follow the teaching of this passage. I can draw near with a true heart, because a true heart is one that trusts the Lord. A trusting heart is a heart full of assurance that remembers, as my wife, Pat, declared about our move to California, "God will take care of us."

You will keep in perfect peace him whose mind is steadfast, because he trusts in you.

–Isaiah 26:3

Do not be anxious about anything, but in everything, by prayer and petition, with thanksgiving, present your requests to God. And the peace of God, which transcends all understanding, will guard your hearts and yours minds in Christ Jesus.

–Philippians 4:6-7

Pray, asking God to enable you to have full assurance that He will keep you in His care.

Summary Points to Ponder

- When you lose your trust, you lose your hope.
- When you lose your hope, you lose your heart for ministry.
- Trust the Lord with your whole heart.
- When you trust the Lord with all your heart, assurance results.
- Trusting the Lord brings security to your heart.

Week 2, Day 4

PLEASING GOD – THE AMBITION OF THE HEART

This Week

Day 1: Knowing God – The Relationship of the Heart
Day 2: Seeking God – The Activity of the Heart
Day 3: Trusting God – The Security of the Heart
Day 4: Pleasing God – The Ambition of the Heart
Day 5: Following God – The Response of the Heart

At age 10, my daughter, Mary, worked hard to improve her batting score for her softball team. She wanted to make sure she could hit the ball and not embarrass herself by striking out. Every evening we went to the batting cage to practice. Mary really put her heart into working on her batting skills.

In one of her early games, she had two strikes against her, with runners in scoring position. The pressure was definitely on! The pitcher threw a hard pitch right down the middle of the plate, and Mary hit the ball for a double! As she stopped at second base, she looked over at her mother and me. She wanted to make sure that we were pleased with her hitting. I believe that it meant as much to her that we were pleased as it did to her that she hit the double. Children love their parents' approval. They want their parents to be pleased with them and their actions.

Your Great Ambition

If you are to keep your heart in ministry, aim at pleasing your heavenly Father. The great ambition of each heart must be to please God. The apostle Paul modeled this principle and encouraged others to do so. He said to the Corinthian church, "So we must make it our goal to please him, whether we are at home in the body or away from it" (2 Corinthians 5:9).

It is both easy, and very human, to be drawn into the habit of pleasing others rather than God. Consider the experience of this leader.

> When I started my career in leadership, my burning desire was to be liked by others. During my first two years of ministry, nearly everything I did was motivated by my goal to please people and win them over to me personally.
>
> But then God dealt with me on that issue. I began visiting a man in the hospital who was the brother of a woman in my church. Each day for a week we'd chat about the Cincinnati Reds or some other unimportant topic. He was a nice guy, and I enjoyed talking to him. I think he really liked me.

> Then one day a few hours after I had visited him, I got the call that he had died. And I realized that he had gone to the grave without ever hearing me share my faith. I was devastated. I had cared more about his opinion of me than about the condition of his soul.
>
> For months I wrestled with the memory of my indifference to that man. It was one of the lowest points of my life. It truly broke me, and God was able to deal with me and turn my heart toward Him.
>
> That incident changed my life forever. I decided that I would dedicate myself to what was truly important. Just as it had for Deborah, God's mission became my mission. And I dedicated the remainder of my life to building God's kingdom, not my reputation.[1]

Whether Paul lived or died, he wanted his life to please God. In my ministry, I often have placed my personal ambition above pleasing the Lord. My way and my desires often seemed most important. Whether your ministry condition at the moment is fruitful or unfruitful, your desire can be to please God. If God wants to use you in a hard, seemingly unfruitful ministry, then be willing to please Him. Paul reminded Timothy to suffer hardship as a good soldier of Jesus Christ. He also encouraged him to remember how soldiers separate themselves and live under discipline in order to please the one who recruited them (see 2 Timothy 2:3-4 at right.)

Endure hardship with us like a good soldier of Christ Jesus. No one serving as a soldier gets involved in civilian affairs—he wants to please his commanding officer.
—2 Timothy 2:3-4

A missionary felt called to serve in an area of North Africa where the law does not allow people to tell about Jesus. He was not permitted to work in the country to which he felt called, so he and his family lived across the border and ministered to people from the restricted country as they visited the area where he lived. His desire was that they learn about Jesus and then return to their homeland to multiply believers there. Despite several years of determined effort, he saw few converts because of the fear of reprisal when the visitors returned to their native land. The years of hard, seemingly unfruitful ministry would have discouraged many people. But this missionary was not deterred from his goal to preach the gospel to people who had never heard. When asked how he kept going, the missionary spoke of his desire to please God instead of focusing on visible successes or failures.

Week 2, Day 4

PLEASING GOD – THE AMBITION OF THE HEART *continued . . .*

What has been your experience in this area? Have you ever served God in a ministry that seemed unproductive and unfruitful? If so, describe below. ____
____
____
____

What encouraged you to keep going? Was it another's counsel, a particular passage of Scripture, a message you heard, a book you read, or some other means of inspiration? Describe here. ________________________________
____
____
____

17-I know, my God, that you test the heart and are pleased with integrity. All these things have I given willingly and with honest intent. And now I have seen with joy how willingly your people who are here have given to you.

18-O Lord, God of our fathers Abraham, Isaac and Israel, keep this desire in the hearts of your people forever, and keep their hearts loyal to you.

19-And give my son Solomon the wholehearted devotion to keep your commands, requirements and decrees and to do everything to build the palatial structure for which I have provided.

–1 Chronicles 29:17-19

A Heart that Pleases God

Perhaps you're at that crossroads in your life right now. Your work for God — teaching a Sunday School class, serving as a deacon, pastoring, serving as a staff member or denominational employee — seems extremely difficult, so difficult that you wonder if you can go on. If this is true of you now, consider David's example.

As you know, David was a man after God's own heart. He sought to please God with his whole heart. When he was preparing to turn the throne over to his son Solomon, he brought the people of Israel together and prayed for God's blessing on Solomon and his work in building the temple and leading the people (see 1 Chronicles 29:17-19 in the margin). Through his prayer, David also taught the people some valuable lessons about keeping their hearts set on pleasing God.

Below is a list of lessons that David taught the people in his prayer. Write the number of the verse from the passage beside the lesson David taught.

_____ 1. God tests your heart.
_____ 2. God is pleased when you live in uprightness (integrity).
_____ 3. David told the Lord that he had served him with an upright heart.

_____ 4. As a result, he led God's people to willingly offer their resources to build the temple.
_____ 5. He asked God to fix or set the people's heart toward God.
_____ 6. He asked God to give to Solomon a loyal heart, one that would seek to please God throughout his reign as king.

In this prayer David expresses the desires of a heart that seeks to please God. (I'm sure you saw that the first four statements related to verse 17, the fifth to verse 18, and the last to verse 19.) Do not seek to please God with your actions; first give Him your heart, and the rest will follow (see Proverbs 23:26 in the right margin). God is pleased when you trust Him with your heart. Your ministry will be stronger. The people to whom you minister will be better when you lead, keeping your heart by making it your aim to first please God.

My son, give me your heart and let your eyes keep to my ways.
–Proverbs 23:26

Stop for a time of prayer. Ask God to search your heart and reveal to you any times in which you've concentrated on achieving certain goals more than on having a heart solely devoted to pleasing Him. Confess these instances to Him. Ask God to help you keep your eyes on Him in the future.

Summary Points to Ponder

- Your ambition must be to please God, and this ambition springs from your heart.
- God will test your heart to see if you desire to please Him.
- God is pleased when you live in holiness and uprightness.
- All other ambitions must be secondary to pleasing God.

1 John C. Maxwell, *The 21 Most Powerful Minutes in a Leader's Day* (Nashville: Thomas Nelson Publishers, 2000), 112.

Week 2, Day 5

FOLLOWING GOD – THE RESPONSE OF THE HEART

This Week

As a minister's mate, my wife, Pat, has had to live in some incredibly difficult places. In my first pastorate, we lived in a small, white house next to the church. Although it once had been a parsonage for the ministers there, it had evolved into a storage shed for items such as tools, pipes, and old furniture.

I was so excited to be the new minister of the church that I wanted to get out and live with the people in the "field." When I showed Pat our new home, the expression on her face was unforgettable, as she surveyed that dwelling. She looked around at the broken-out windows, the trash that had blown in from the outside, the junk that littered the rooms, and the bathroom where the floor had rotted away. She swallowed hard and said, "Honey, when I agreed to marry you, I didn't think it would be like this, but I'm ready to live here if this is what you want us to do!"

My wife's willingness to follow me to this run-down house as we began our first pastorate illustrates how to keep your heart in ministry. Keep in your heart a willing response to follow God wherever He leads.

A Different Spirit Within Him

The biblical character Caleb illustrates how vital it is to keep your heart by following God. Caleb was one of the original spies who looked over the land God promised to Israel. When the spies returned with their report that the walls were too high and the people were too big for Israel to defeat, Caleb called on the people to have faith in God and to follow him into the land (See Numbers 14:6-9 in the left and far right margins). Despite the people's refusal to enter the land, God promised that Joshua and Caleb would be allowed to enter. God saw something different in Caleb and Joshua. God said of Caleb, "But because my servant Caleb has a different spirit and follows me wholeheartedly, I will bring him into the land he went to, and his descendants will inherit it" (Numbers 14:24). Following God starts in the heart. It requires a different spirit to keep focused on following God.

Joshua son of Nun and Caleb son of Jephunneh, who were among those who had explored the land, tore their clothes and said to the entire Israelite assembly, "The land we passed through and explored is exceedingly good. If the Lord is pleased with us, he will lead us into that land, a land flowing with milk and honey, and will give it to us.

–Numbers 14:6-8

(Continued on next page...)

What kind of "different spirit" do you have that keeps you following God? Check any of the statements below that you believe describe you, or write in your own answer. Put an asterisk by any that may not currently describe you but which you may have as a goal for your life.

- ❑ I try to make room for my daily quiet time regardless of how busy or tired I am.
- ❑ I try to keep my focus on God and His desires for me rather than on my current circumstances.
- ❑ I try to maintain discipline in my personal life and to avoid habits, places, or individuals that are harmful influences on me.
- ❑ I try not to hold grudges or dwell on slights that could keep me preoccupied with people rather than on serving God.
- ❑ I confess individual sins as quickly as possible and ask God to forgive me.
- ❑ Other ____

Only do not rebel against the Lord. And do not be afraid of the people of the land, because we will swallow them up. Their protection is gone, but the Lord is with us. Do not be afraid of them.
–Numbers 14:9

A Reputation for Following God

Caleb developed a reputation for following God. When some 40 years later he met again with Joshua to receive the part of the land that was promised for his descendants, he reminded Joshua of God's promise to him (Joshua 14:6-12). He remained faithful in following God. In fact, at the end of his life, he asked for the greatest challenge of all. He wanted the mountain where the giants lived (see Joshua 14:12 in the margin). He believed that as he followed God, He could defeat the giants and conquer the land.

At his life's end, Caleb was known as a man who followed God. The Bible's final words about Caleb read "because he [Caleb] followed the Lord, the God of Israel, wholeheartedly" (Joshua 14:14).

Visualize this being said about you. Put your name in the blank below.
"Because ______________________________ followed the Lord, the God of Israel, wholeheartedly."

Now give me this hill country that the Lord promised me that day. You yourself heard then that the Anakites were there and their cities were large and fortified, but, the Lord helping me, I will drive them out just as he said.
–Joshua 14:12

Week 2, Day 5

FOLLOWING GOD – THE RESPONSE OF THE HEART *continued . . .*

Notes

If this statement can't be honestly made about you right now, what stands in the way? Describe what keeps you from following God wholeheartedly.

____

____

____

____

____

Make the response of your heart to follow God — wherever and whatever He calls you to do. In ministry you will face many obstacles, troubles, and challenges, but like Caleb, *keep your heart by wholly following God wherever He leads.*

Pray about these matters. Ask God to remove any obstacles that keep you from following Him with a whole heart.

Summary Points to Ponder

- Following God wholeheartedly is built on your faith in God.
- Following God wholeheartedly starts on the inside.
- Following God wholeheartedly keeps your heart from fear.
- Following God wholeheartedly is honored by God.
- Following God wholeheartedly will keep your heart in ministry.

Week 3, Introduction

KEEPING YOUR HEART FOR THE KINGDOM

I have always treasured a special gift that my father gave me — my great-grandfather's pocket watch. The watch occupies a spot on the bookshelf in my study. Whenever I look at it, it reminds me that I am part of a family. It reminds me that I represent a family name and a history.

I would never want to do anything to shame my family name. My great-grandfather's watch reminds me of the gift of my heritage. The fact that I am part of a family is a gift I can never lose.

Jesus said, "Do not fear, little flock, for it is the Father's good pleasure to give you the kingdom" (Luke 12:32, NKJV). God the Father has given His children the kingdom. Think of it! You are part of the kingdom of God! Your position in the kingdom is a gift from God — far more precious than the pocket watch I hold so dear.

Thinking about being given the kingdom excites and motivates me. Jesus focused His teachings on the kingdom of God. He spoke more often of the kingdom than of the church. Recognizing this position spurs me on to keep my heart for the kingdom.

What about you today — are you keeping your heart for the kingdom? Are you ready to serve God wherever He may place you in His kingdom work?

Read Matthew 6:33 appearing in the margin. What place does "seeking his kingdom" hold in relationship to other things you do in life?

____

____

____

Jesus did not command that you seek His kingdom whenever you feel like it. He did not command that you seek His kingdom after all your other wishes and desires are met. He commanded that you seek it first — it is to be your top priority.

Seek the kingdom with your whole heart. The kingdom is your prize — the pearl of great price. This week's study will focus on several important ways that you can work to keep your heart for the kingdom.

This Week

Day 1: Focusing on the Right Priority
Day 2: Paying Attention to Your Heart
Day 3: Staying Prepared for Your Work
Day 4: Staying Pure in Heart
Day 5: Staying Transparent

But seek first his kingdom and his righteousness, and all these things will be given to you as well.
–Matthew 6:33

Week 3, Day 1

FOCUSING ON THE RIGHT PRIORITY

This Week

Our family's dog, Rebel, has lots of toys. If you visited us and didn't know us well, you would think we were parents of a preschooler because toys are scattered all over the living room. These toys belong to our dog!

When I play with Rebel, I'm always amazed at his short attention span. If I begin to play with him by throwing a ball, he runs to retrieve the ball several times, but after only a few minutes, he becomes distracted. He looks around and sees another of his toys, drops the ball, and begins to play with the new toy. He does this again and again because Rebel has absolutely no focus.

This story illustrates the fact that to keep your heart, you must maintain your focus on God's priorities. A short attention span invariably robs you of focus — so ask for God's help as you determine to align your priorities with His. To seek the kingdom of God and His righteousness, you must start with the right heart *focus*.

What kinds of things distract you or rob you of focus in your ministry? Check any below that apply, or add your own.

- ❑ Interpersonal conflicts
- ❑ Financial worries
- ❑ Personal achievement
- ❑ Others' criticisms of you
- ❑ Inability to say no/overwork
- ❑ Desire for material possessions
- ❑ Lack of organization/good work habits
- ❑ Desire for others' approval
- ❑ Other ______________________________

I have found that when my schedule becomes increasingly heavy with personal and work commitments, I become distracted. I allow the tyranny of the urgent to push aside the important spiritual issues of life. My heart is distracted; I fail to keep my heart.

On one occasion, I faced the distraction of opposition. Two church members that I counted as good friends began to spread untruths about me and my ministry as their pastor. Their opposition devastated me. It took a long time for me to recover from that time of opposition. I finally realized that the opposition had distracted me from my walk with God and had stolen both my heart and the joy I had in my ministry.

Paul faced a similar situation when untruths were spread about his ministry. He recognized the potential impact of diverting his attention away from his God-directed mission. He also saw how the overall work could be hindered by these untruths. Paul moved quickly and decisively to expose his detractors' motives and returned his focus to the work at hand.

One layperson I know excels in leading small discipleship groups at her church. The term of her groups usually extends from September through June, with a break for the summer. She comments that in the summer, she always yearns for September to arrive because her patterns of consistent witnessing, Scripture memorization, and ministry to others improve when she is part of the regular regimen of group life and accountability to others. She complains about how vulnerable she is to becoming distracted with other demands, losing her focus on the kingdom of God as a consequence.

We proclaim him, admonishing and teaching everyone with all wisdom, so that we may present everyone perfect in Christ. To this end I labor, struggling with all his energy, which so powerfully works in me.
–Colossians 1:28-29

Focus on Things Above
No other New Testament writer is as open about his own leadership struggles and feelings as is the apostle Paul. In Colossians, chapter one, and particularly verses 28-29, he relates how he was able to maintain his focus on the kingdom of God.

Since, then, you have been raised with Christ, set your hearts on things above, where Christ is seated at the right hand of God. Set your minds on things above, not on earthly things.
–Colossians 3:1-2

Read Colossians 3:1-2 in the margin. With two lines underline the words that indicate where Paul admonishes you to set your heart. With one line, underline the words which describe where Paul tells you to avoid setting your heart.

Why is this focus so important? Focusing on things above, not on earthly things, is crucial because that is where Christ "is seated at the right hand of God," as verse 1 reminds you.

So we fix our eyes not on what is seen, but on what is unseen. For what is seen is temporary, but what is unseen is eternal.
–2 Corinthians 4:18

To keep my heart in ministry, I cannot afford to become distracted, like my little dog Rebel, with all the things that surround me. I must keep my focus on things above, where Christ sits as King. My heart must be attached to the unseen (see 2 Corinthians 4:18 at right) — the things above that God has given to me. I must remember that Christ is on His throne; He is sovereign

Week 3, Day 1

FOCUSING ON THE RIGHT PRIORITY

continued . . .

Lord and ruler of all things. My heart and yours can be strong because Christ sits at the right hand of God.

Preoccupied with God's Kingdom
When you observe the life of the apostle Paul, you quickly see that he was preoccupied with the kingdom of God. Whatever he did or wherever he went, he couldn't stop talking about the kingdom of God. It was the overwhelming focus of his life and ministry. As a church planter, evangelist, and pastor, he kept his focus on the kingdom of God.

Now I know that none of you among whom I have gone about preaching the kingdom will ever see me again.
–Acts 20:25

As he left his dear brothers the Ephesians, he reminded them that his entire ministry with them had been one of speaking and teaching on the kingdom of God (see Acts 20:25 in the margin). As Paul closed his ministry, his focus continued to be Jesus Christ and the kingdom of God. In Acts 28:30-31, Luke writes of Paul, "For two whole years Paul stayed there in his own rented house and welcomed all who came to see him. Boldly and without hindrance he preached the kingdom of God and taught about the Lord Jesus Christ."

Now that is keeping your heart focused on the right priority!

Can you think of a time when you were so focused on the kingdom that you couldn't stop talking about Christ? Perhaps this occurred when you were a new Christian or during a period when Christ was particularly real to you. Perhaps it happened when you were involved in an especially rewarding ministry. Regardless of when it occurred, describe such a time here.

____

____

____

____

Stop and pray, asking God to give you a singular focus on Him, so that you can't stop talking about His role in your life. Ask the Holy Spirit to keep this matter before you daily.

Summary Points to Ponder

- Keeping your heart means focusing on God's priority — the kingdom.
- Seek those things that are above where Christ is seated.
- When you fix your heart on the kingdom, you will be consumed by the reality of the kingdom of God.
- When you set your focus on the kingdom, it will dominate your conversation and your actions!

Notes

Week 3, Day 2

PAYING ATTENTION TO YOUR HEART

This Week

Watch your life and doctrine closely. Persevere in them, because if you do, you will save both yourself and your hearers.
–1 Timothy 4:16

A college roommate of mine was the most meticulous person I have ever met. One Monday I returned from a trip to my weekend church. When I opened the door, I saw, to my surprise, that Bob had antiqued our dormitory room furniture! In addition, both beds now had matching bedspreads. Bob was so concerned about these details that he had spared no effort in making sure that the room was absolutely picture perfect. Looking back, I must confess that I haven't always been as careful about keeping my heart as Bob was in keeping that room in tip-top shape.

Caring for My Spiritual Condition
In 1 Timothy 4:16, Paul urged Timothy: "Watch your life and doctrine closely." If I am to keep my heart focused on the kingdom of God, I must become meticulous about caring for my spiritual condition.

I will not be of much use in my ministry if my heart is pulled away from its focus on the kingdom work that God has given me to do. Solomon said, "Who can say, 'I have kept my heart pure; I am clean and without sin'?" (Proverbs 20:9). By nature, we are prone to sin. Keeping my heart (and yours) pure requires careful diligence.

A Bible study leader told me this week he was teaching a new stewardship study in a small group. As he prepared to teach, he discovered much to his surprise, that he really loves money. He said, "I had never really come to grips with it. But as I studied, there it was. I had several conversations with the Lord that week, driving up and down the freeway. I've asked Him to help me put money in proper perspective." He went on to relate that on many occasions, preparing to teach a subject has caused him to face a heart condition that had previously gone unnoticed.

The best way to purify your heart is to pay careful attention to what is in your heart.

What are some things in your life that, in the past, have served as warning signs to you that your heart was unclean and that you had strayed

from a righteous path? Below, check all that apply, or add your own ideas.

- ❑ I'm holding anger or a grudge against someone else.
- ❑ I find myself reading materials which express views that do not conform to the teachings of Christ.
- ❑ Bible study revealed an area of concern.
- ❑ My conversations sometimes contain off-color expressions, improper humor, or biting sarcasm.
- ❑ I listen to unclean jokes and do not object or immediately remove myself from a conversation in which such jokes are being told.
- ❑ I find myself speaking harshly or critically to friends or family members.
- ❑ I find myself listening to, or participating in, gossip or conversation that would be hurtful to others.
- ❑ I discover that I'm failing to discriminate in my television viewing and am spending more and more time watching programs that do not uphold strong moral values.
- ❑ I am thinking more of acquiring "stuff" than I am of seeking the kingdom.
- ❑ Other ____

Your thoughts and your words clearly reveal what is in your heart. Keep your heart by monitoring carefully every word that comes from your mouth and by being alert to harmful thoughts that can lead to actions that divert you from your ministry.

Stop and pray, asking God to keep you alert to anything unclean in your heart that will pull your heart away from kingdom work. Invite His Holy Spirit to examine your heart right now, probing for things you may have overlooked.

Watching for a Deceitful Heart

When Moses warned the children of Israel about the blessings or obedience and the curses of disobeying God, he said, "Be careful, or you will be enticed to turn away and worship other gods and bow down to them" (Deuteronomy

Notes

Week 3, Day 2

PAY ATTENTION TO YOUR HEART *continued . . .*

Rend your heart and not your garments. Return to the Lord your God, for he is gracious and compassionate, slow to anger and abounding in love, and he relents from sending calamity
–Joel 2:13

11:16). David gave a similar admonition when he said, "Though your riches increase, do not set your heart on them" (Psalm 62:10).

Your task of keeping your heart for the kingdom requires that you pay attention so that you do not develop a heart that deceives you. When your heart deceives you, you lose your spiritual sensitivities. You stop thinking about God's purposes and priorities. When your heart deceives you, do what Zechariah called the people to do (see Joel 2:13 in the margin).

Below check any of the statements that describe ways your heart has, or you feel has the potential to, deceive you in your ministry and keep you from kingdom work.

- ❑ I become so consumed with the demands of my roles and leadership position that I neglect my physical health (fail to exercise, eat improperly, get insufficient rest or relaxation.)
- ❑ I become so consumed with the demands of my roles and leadership position that I neglect the needs of my spouse, children, parents, or friends.
- ❑ I become so satisfied with my church's/Sunday School class'/church committee's growth that I fail to pay attention to members' personal needs.
- ❑ I become haughty and prideful because of my accomplishments as a leader and fail to remain humble and responsive to God's direction in my life.
- ❑ I fail to set proper relational boundaries when I visit, counsel, or interact with members of the opposite gender and therefore become vulnerable to an improper relationship.
- ❑ I become caught up in the prestige of the leadership role that I hold and forget about the servant spirit that God requires of leaders.
- ❑ I forget the difference between God and myself — trying to be the ultimate controller/micromanager of all outcomes.
- ❑ I try to perform my ministry in my own strength and forget that the strength of God and God alone empowers me.
- ❑ Other ____

____

____

Notes

I can keep my heart focused on the kingdom only as I pay attention to my heart! All leaders are vulnerable. Don't cooperate with the evil one by failing to regularly assess your heart.

As you consider the above descriptions, or any you may have added, stop and pray. Confess your sin to God and pray fervently that He will halt you anytime you allow your heart to be deceived in the future. Ask His Holy Spirit to reveal any area where you may not see yourself as you really are.

Summary Points to Ponder

- My responsibility as a believer in ministry is to pay attention to my heart.
- When I watch my heart, I keep myself prepared for kingdom work.
- My thoughts, motives, and actions flow out of my heart and reveal what is there.
- When I allow deceit to creep into my heart, I am unable to keep a kingdom focus.

Week 3, Day 3

STAYING PREPARED FOR YOUR WORK

This Week

From my longtime friend, Randy, who is a captain in the fire department, I have learned a valuable lesson about staying prepared. Randy is immensely dedicated to his work. I have watched him leave his family, risking his life to fight wildfires in the California mountains. He has a passion for his job, and it shows in how he performs.

Randy is also an outstanding athlete. He competed in the fireman olympics and finished second overall in the nation! I asked Randy what he believes is the key to being an effective firefighter. He replied, "Always be prepared!" Firefighters never know when they will be called on to face an emergency. Through training and discipline they must prepare to face whatever situation is handed them.

In the same way, when I prepare my heart and maintain my focus on the kingdom, I can meet the challenges of the work that God has given me to do.

A Prepared Heart

Scripture teaches that you can prepare your heart for your work. When you meditate on the truths of God's Word, you become prepared for what God has called you to do. David said, "My heart grew hot within me; and as I meditated, the fire burned" (Psalm 39:3). When the Lord spoke to Joshua, He reminded him of the tremendous value of meditation.

Be strong and very courageous. Be careful to obey all the law my servant Moses gave you; do not turn from it to the right or to the left, that you may be successful wherever you go. Do not let this Book of the Law depart from your mouth; meditate on it day and night, so that you may be careful to do everything written in it. Then you will be prosperous and successful.
–Joshua 1:7-8

A coworker was preparing for a mission trip to Scotland. She had been warned that witnessing opportunities there would be different from her past experiences in other parts of the world. She prayed that God would give her a great love for the people she encountered. Just a matter of days before departure, she read a passage in John that immediately gave both an answer, and the peace she had been seeking. "You did not choose me, but I chose you and appointed you to go and to bear fruit — fruit that will last. Then the Father will give you whatever you ask in my name" (John 15:16).

Read Joshua 1:7-8 in the margin. Underline the assurance that God gave Joshua if he would meditate on His Word.

The Lord promised Joshua that he would flourish and succeed in his leadership task if he meditated on the Law and then was careful to follow through by doing the things He learned. Likewise, you can rest on God's promise that He will bless your hiding His Word in your heart so you can act on what it tells you to do.

Think about a time when a particular Scripture that you have pondered and tucked away in your heart has helped you to succeed as a leader. In these blanks, mention the verse and tell how it helped you.

____

____

____

For example, in my life, I have found Philippians 3:10 to be a particularly important verse to have memorized as I went through my ministry tasks. In this verse, Paul wrote, "I want to know Christ and the power of his resurrection and the fellowship of sharing in his sufferings, becoming like him in his death." Paul's three-fold desire to know Christ keeps me motivated. I know I haven't attained or achieved the spiritual growth that I need, but I desire, like Paul, to know Him in His fullness! This verse has always strengthened me in my ministry journey.

A Hot Heart

When Jeremiah faced ridicule and mistreatment for speaking the truth of God's Word, he became so discouraged he thought he would not speak for the Lord anymore. (Read Jeremiah 20:9 in the margin.)

But if I say, "I will not mention him or speak any more in his name," his word is in my heart like a fire, a fire shut up in my bones. I am weary of holding it in; indeed, I cannot.
–Jeremiah 20:9

Have you ever felt as Jeremiah said he did, as recorded in the first part of this verse? Have you ever been so discouraged that you wondered how you could continue in your ministry task? ❑ Yes ❑ No If you answered yes, describe the situation.

____

____

Many people can identify with the depths of Jeremiah's discouragement. However, because Jeremiah had prepared himself as God's messenger, he went on to say that God's Word was like a fire shut up in his bones that he couldn't possibly hold back!

Week 3, Day 3

STAYING PREPARED FOR YOUR WORK

continued . . .

A friend of mine shares this story:

> I served as administrator of a large Christian school, facing a major budget crisis. The school board and I agonized over what actions to take. The decision was made to reduce staff by 25% and to make cuts in other areas.
>
> Our board met with the faculty, told them of the situation, and promised that I would personally talk to each teacher affected – 21 of them – by the end of the next school day.
>
> Immediately, I began receiving angry, abusive phone calls hardly befitting any Christian. One night my wife answered the phone and almost immediately hung up, in tears. A man had actually threatened my life. Worse, my daughter asked her mother if it was true that I had fired her teacher so that her mother could keep her job in the library. One of my daughter's teachers had made this accusation.
>
> It is one thing when leadership responsibilities result in criticism, but when it extends to your wife and children, it tears your heart to shreds. During this time, one verse became very dear to my heart. It was the verse in Peter that tells us to "Cast all your anxiety on him because he cares for you" (1 Peter 5:7).
>
> God brought me through this difficult time, and I enjoyed a wonderful tenure at this school. Some of the very teachers who were so hurtful were brought back on staff when finances allowed, yet not one ever apologized for what was said nor for attitudes displayed earlier. Because of the grace of God I could totally forgive them and leave each one in God's hand. Without Him at my side and His calling sure in my heart, I might not have survived.

Endure hardship with us like a good soldier of Christ Jesus. No one serving as a soldier gets involved in civilian affairs—he wants to please his commanding officer.
—2 Timothy 2:3-4

When you prepare yourself for kingdom work, God sets your heart on fire. Like Jeremiah, you will not be able to keep from speaking for Him! Paul reminded Timothy to prepare like a soldier for battle (see 2 Timothy 2:3-4 in the margin.) As a leader, prepare your heart through meditation and prayer for the kingdom work God has specifically called you to do.

In my own life, my time with God has always been a challenge. Probably like you have, I have tried different methods. What seems to have worked best for me through the years is to read each day from the Psalms and Proverbs and spend time focused on key Scripture passages for meditation. I have a prayer list that begins with self-evaluation and moves outward to praying for my coworkers, family, and other needs.

Whatever your pattern is of having a daily time to meditate, don't minimize the importance of this critical step to keep your heart hot and prepared.

Pray about this very subject. Ask God to keep your heart always prepared for His kingdom work. If you are married, you might want to ask your spouse to pray specifically for you on this matter. If you are single, consider asking this of a close friend.

Summary Points to Ponder

- Preparation is essential for effective kingdom ministers.
- Meditation and prayer prepare you for your kingdom work.
- Discouragements and busyness can hinder kingdom work.
- A prepared heart is a hot heart for God's kingdom work.

Notes

Week 3, Day 4

STAYING PURE IN HEART

This Week

One of the most difficult things to witness is the destruction of a friend's ministry. I once sat with a pastor friend while he met with his deacons to explain the causes of his moral failure. He asked them to forgive him for how he had devastated the work of the church because of his immorality and lack of integrity.

As he sat weeping before the church leadership, he confessed, "This has happened because I didn't stay pure." His words cut like a knife into my heart. Although I certainly had not been guilty of moral infidelity toward my wife, I realized my heart hadn't always been pure.

Purity and Happiness
In the Sermon on the Mount, Jesus outlined the characteristics of a kingdom disciple. He taught His disciples the absolute importance of a pure heart. Jesus said, "Blessed are the pure in heart, for they will see God" (Matthew 5:8). According to the Lord, the pure in heart are happy. Ministry done in purity of heart is a happy, fulfilling, satisfying ministry. When you are pure in heart, Jesus promises you will see God. There are certain things that can only been seen by the pure in heart — pure at the very core of your being.

The goal of this command is love, which comes from a pure heart and a good conscience and a sincere faith.
—1 Timothy 1:5

Purity and Love
When Paul instructed Timothy in how he was to conduct himself as a minister, he taught him that love comes from a pure heart. See what he said about this in 1 Timothy 1:5 in the margin.

A woman told of an experience she had many years ago while serving in a small church in southern Illinois. She wanted to support her minister husband and was very committed to both teaching and the children's choir ministries in their church. She felt pressured to lead one of the women's missionary study groups and also spent a considerable amount of time visiting the local nursing homes. The couple had three young children, all involved in various church and school activities.

Finding no time for herself, and barely able to meet the demands of church and home, she found herself becoming increasingly irritable and eventually resentful. There was little love in what she was doing. She finally came to understand that too many activities can crowd God out of the most committed heart. She discovered that God does not place overwhelming demands on His children. She learned (the hard way!) to pray over each request, confirming God's plan and purpose for her ministry. Keeping her heart pure before God allowed her to minister effectively and lovingly.

The goal of teaching and ministering to the people of God is love from a pure heart. Jesus is able to love you because His heart is pure. In doing the kingdom work that God has called me to carry out, like Him, I must maintain a pure heart. Without it, I lose my love for the people God has called me to serve.

Reread the last two sentences in the above paragraph. Below, check statements that describe ways that an impure heart could cause you to lose your love for those you lead.

- ❑ I can become so focused on success (increasing membership numbers, innovative programs, building expansion, etc.) that I forget to pay attention to people and their needs.
- ❑ I can become so vain about my speaking abilities and so prideful about people's compliments of me that I forget to speak God's message and the words that He lays on my heart for people to hear.
- ❑ I can focus so much on laying foundations for getting ahead in the future that I fail to be a servant of the Lord and of His people today.
- ❑ I can delude myself by thinking that I'm immune from lustful thoughts or from sexual temptation rather than constantly remaining aware of my vulnerability and constantly asking God to bind Satan in my life.
- ❑ I fail to seek God's plan for kingdom ministry and dilute my efforts with busyness.
- ❑ I can grow covetous of others' churches, Sunday School classes, or committee assignments and allow that envy to sap my energy rather than staying focused on the current group of believers God has given me to shepherd/disciple.
- ❑ Other ____
  ____

Notes

Week 3, Day 4

STAYING PURE IN HEART *continued . . .*

O Lord Almighty, you who examine the righteous and probe the heart and mind.
–Jeremiah 20:12

Purity and Prayer
Your heart can also become impure when you become convinced of your self-sufficiency and importance and forget to pray, asking God to search your mind and heart. Read, in the margin, how Jeremiah addressed God in Jeremiah 20:12, Jeremiah addressed God as the "Lord Almighty, you who examine the righteous and probe the heart and mind."

Think of it — God knows your heart and mind! He knows what you think about. He is aware of the deep matters that hide away in your heart that no one else can see. He knows about the times when you allow your mind to dwell on a scene from a sexually explicit television show you stumbled onto. He knows about the times when you patted yourself on the back for the great discipleship course you taught and failed to give Him and Him alone the credit for the members' growth. He knows about the time you envied a neighbor because of his new car and the time you thought something unkind about a fellow church member. He knows about the time you held a grudge because of someone's slight and were vengeful because you didn't get your way. He knows about the promises you have failed to keep, the snap judgements you've made, or gossip you've spread without checking out the facts.

Even if you think all these failings are private and are hidden from others' view, God knows about them. He grieves because He knows the impact your impure heart has on your ministry. Impurity of heart keeps you from serving with joy and gladness. It creates guilt that burdens you and keeps you from happiness and fulfillment in your areas of service. Impurity limits your effectiveness in the kingdom.

Can you identify with any of the descriptions mentioned above? If so, underline one or more that describe something of which you've been guilty. Below, tell how one of these examples of impurity has hindered you from serving with happiness and fulfillment.

____

____

____

____

Never forget, however, that you have an Advocate Who was tempted in all ways as we are, yet without sin (see Hebrews 4:15 in the margin). Your Advocate will intercede for you! Call on Him, and He will respond to your need. As a kingdom minister, pray fervently to God about these matters. When your heart is pure, you will call on God, and He will hear you. Paul said, "flee the evil desires of youth, and pursue righteousness, faith, love and peace, along with those who call on the Lord out of a pure heart" (2 Timothy 2:22).

For we do not have a high priest who is unable to sympathize with our weaknesses, but we have one who has been tempted in every way, just as we are – yet was without sin.
–Hebrews 4:15

Purity keeps my heart for the kingdom.

Get on your knees before the Lord. Ask Him to show you areas of impurity on which you need to work. Perhaps at this stage in your study, you need to find an accountability partner, if you don't have one already. Ask this person to help you remain accountable for thoughts or acts of impurity that would harm your ministry.

Summary Points to Ponder

- When my heart is pure, I am happy and fulfilled in my ministry.
- When my heart is pure, my ministry is expressed in love.
- When my heart is pure, I can speak to God out of pure motives.
- I have an Advocate Who cares for me and Who will help me become pure in heart.

Week 3, Day 5

STAYING TRANSPARENT

This Week

Day 1: Focusing on the Right Priority
Day 2: Paying Attention to Your Heart
Day 3: Staying Prepared for Your Work
Day 4: Staying Pure in Heart
Day 5: Staying Transparent

One of the attributes I appreciate most in a minister is transparency — the behavior and actions of a minister that allows you to see into the soul of the person. You feel as if you understand the person and understand the point from where the individual is coming. Too often as I've ministered, I have done my work from behind a mask. I was too wounded or afraid to merely be myself, no matter what others might think of me.

When I was growing up, my youth minister taught me about transparency. He hid nothing in his life from his youth group. We saw him in the midst of his struggles as well as his joys. I saw him when he was angry and also saw him on his knees before God. I watched his relationship with his wife. He had a profound impact on many. A number of young people were called to the ministry under his influence. I believe his transparency accounted for his tremendous contribution as a kingdom leader. Today, in his fifties, he is still ministering effectively — still transparent! Transparency in the ministry keeps your heart for the kingdom work that God has called you to do.

Have you known persons in ministry like this? Perhaps it was a staff member or Bible-study teacher when you were growing up, or someone who is influential in your life today. If so, write the person or persons' initials here. In a brief sentence describe what you remember about this leader's transparency that impacted you. Thank God for this person's influence on your life.

___

___

___

A Lowly Heart

Jesus modeled the principle of transparency powerfully in His own ministry. He urged, "Take my yoke upon you and learn from me, for I am gentle and humble in heart, and you will find rest for your souls" (Matthew 11:29). A transparent heart is a humble heart. Jesus described His heart as lowly. Jesus was a lowly-hearted minister. No pretense existed in His work. He was an open book to all who saw Him. My kingdom ministry is authenticated by my transparency. I need a lowly heart in order to be transparent.

An Open Heart

God used the apostle Paul greatly in kingdom work. His transparency was clear to all who dealt with him. When Paul speaks in his letters to the churches, an openness and honesty shines through that teaches us about transparency.

For example, the Corinthian church greatly criticized Paul. Yet Paul says to its members, "We have spoken freely to you, Corinthians, and opened wide our hearts to you" (2 Corinthians 6:11). What an incredible statement! "We . . . opened wide our hearts to you," he says. When I read those words, I pause and ask myself, "Am I that transparent in my ministry? Do I allow the people I minister to and with to see my heart?"

A couple from Houston freely share their past failures in marriage. They openly testify of how they allowed worldly influences to destroy their marriages and their Christian influence. They speak of the impact of their actions on their children, now grown. But they also testify to God's healing and forgiveness. Now, some thirty years later, they are a source of counsel and encouragement to other couples, effectively warning them against making the same mistakes. In a large urban church, they could easily choose to remain silent, but they have opted to be transparent.

One Christian leader who comes to mind is highly passionate for the cause of Christ. He feels he is most in the center of God's will when he is traveling from place to place, sacrificing the comforts of home, calling people to serve a lost and dying world. No one could possibly question this leader's call, his motives, or his on-fire spirit for the Lord. But as he speaks, this Christian presents himself as one without flaws. He rarely shares of his own personal struggles or challenges. Despite his earnest passion for God, his unwillingness to appear human causes him to lose credibility. People to whom he speaks see a "super human" before them and think, "I could never possibly be as perfect as this man. Therefore, it will do me no good to try." The impact of his kingdom message is greatly diluted because he declines to be transparent.

I've seen the reverse of this in a couple who conduct marriage-enrichment seminars in church settings. Instead of representing themselves as partners

Notes

Week 3, Day 5

STAYING TRANSPARENT *continued . . .*

Notes

in an ideal marriage, this husband and wife freely share their foibles, their challenges, and the mistakes from which they have learned — including the mistakes they made just last week! Instead of dispensing advice, their approach is to tell how the Lord works in the midst of their difficulties to bring healing and more healthy patterns of communicating. Couples giving feedback say these presenters' transparent way of relating to their audience is the thing that motivates them to work on their marriages.

Below, describe a time when you believe you opened your heart to a person or group to whom you ministered. Describe any positive outcome of this transparency.

____

____

____

Exposing your weaknesses and failings takes courage and involves risk. When I have hidden my heart from others in the past, I have done so because I've been afraid I would be misunderstood or hurt. But a minister with a true heart for the kingdom lives in transparency.

Stop and pray, asking God to give you the courage to be transparent. Ask Him to show you ways that your story of God's grace in the midst of struggle and challenge can be used to help those around you.

Summary Points to Ponder

- Transparency springs from a humble heart.
- Keeping your heart for the kingdom requires transparency.
- Transparency arises out of an open heart.
- Being transparent allows you to minister convincingly and effectively.

Week 4, Introduction

KEEPING YOUR HEART FOR THE CHURCH

I keep a special set of photographs in my desk drawer. They are black and white pictures of an old church building — the first church where I had the privilege to serve as pastor, many years ago. Whenever I forget what God has called me to do in ministry, I take out those pictures as a simple reminder. My heart warms when I recall that when God called me to preach, He gave me a heart for the church.

As imperfect as the church might be, because it is made up of finite human beings, I love the people of God. The photo of my first church reminds me that for more than 100 years, people of God have gathered to worship in that place. My ministry as a kingdom leader is for God's people and those who do not know Him — not for myself. It is all about them!

This week, take time to reflect on this vital principle. Keep your heart for the sake of the church where you serve. Paul expressed this truth several times in his letters to the churches. He wrote to the Corinthians, "All this is for your benefit, so that the grace that is reaching more and more people may cause thanksgiving to overflow to the glory of God" (2 Corinthians 4:16).

Use your study this week to evaluate your love for the church. Love springs from the heart. Perhaps you have experienced trouble in relationship to the church. You may have been disappointed by the actions of certain individuals or in the way a particular issue was handled. We must never lose sight of Jesus' words in Matthew 16:18 (see the verse in the margin). It is *His* church — not mine, not yours, but His church. As parts of the body He calls the church, we are to be mutually supportive, mutually dependent, and collectively characterized by our love for each other. This week of thoughtful study and reflection provides an opportunity for you to recommit your heart to your mission.

This Week

Day 1: Watching for Spiritual Transformation
Day 2: Broken-Hearted Leadership
Day 3: The Power of Relationships
Day 4: No Cost Too High, No Sacrifice Too Great
Day 5: Integrity of Heart and Skillfulness of Hands

And I tell you that you are Peter, and on this rock I will build my church, and the gates of Hades will not overcome it.

-Matthew 16:18

Week 4, Day 1

WATCHING FOR SPIRITUAL TRANSFORMATION

This Week

The first time Willie came to church, he seemed out of place. He lived in a little shack across from the church. The people in the church were uncomfortable with his presence. Willie had lived a difficult life. On his neck was a scar from ear to ear from a knife cut. He had served time — 14 years in San Quentin penitentiary — for killing a man in a fight. Everyone in town knew his story. People were shocked to see him in a house of worship.

However, Willie had recently received Christ as his Lord and Savior. He was a new person. He loved to attend our little church. He had a burning desire to learn the Scriptures. He never missed a service. He once told me, "Since I have become a Christian, the grass looks greener and the sky bluer." Even though he was the first to admit that he didn't have much of a voice, he sometimes asked for permission to get up and sing. He always sang the same song: "Jesus Is the Sweetest Name I Know." He frequently wept before the church. When Willie sang, I realized that situations like his represent what ministry is all about: life transformation.

I am jealous for you with a godly jealousy. I promised you to one husband, to Christ, so that I might present you as a pure virgin to him.
—2 Corinthians 11:2

But I am afraid that just as Eve was deceived by the serpent's cunning, your minds may somehow be led astray from your sincere and pure devotion to Christ.
—2 Corinthians 11:3

Spiritual Jealousy from the Heart

In the letters he wrote, Paul often revealed his heart for the church. At times he was righteously angry, humble, or full of exhortation and instruction, depending on the church's circumstances. In the verse at left, read what he said to the Corinthians. Only as I keep my heart for the church will I share this kind of holy jealousy for God's people and their transformation.

At left, read what Paul went on to say about the church in Corinth. Underline what it was that Paul feared.

Paul feared that the church — Christ's bride — would stray from the path and would serve Him with less than the sincere and pure devotion due the Bridegroom. As God transforms you, and as He transformed Willie, so can He transform the body of believers that you serve, leading them to love others as He loves. Paul demonstrates for you, as ministers and leaders, that only as your hearts are sensitive to the people of God and their spiritual condition can you lead them to Christlikeness.

How can you do this, as Paul admonishes? Below, check some ways that you believe you stay attuned to your members' spiritual condition.

- ❑ Becoming involved with members one-on-one, rather than merely being a figure who "pontificates" and who is not seen as approachable
- ❑ Genuinely listening to members' concerns, rather than absently nodding in assent as they talk with you, hearing what you want to hear when they confide, or quickly cutting them off so you can give advice
- ❑ Avoiding living in denial about the types of moral or spiritual decline that you see among your members, Sunday school classes, church committees, or other groups you lead
- ❑ Seeking the godly counsel of other leaders (if you are a pastor, perhaps this could be another pastor in town or someone whom you respect in another city) about how to deal with sensitive moral issues that exist in your congregation
- ❑ Arranging for Bible studies or group processes that deal with personal issues from a biblical base, so that people who struggle with challenges — such as financial problems, divorce, sexual abuse, painful pasts, or other difficulties that impact them spiritually — can have help from a Christian perspective
- ❑ Other ____

Presenting the Church Complete in Christ

The leader's primary objective is to carry out the Great Commission of the Lord Jesus Christ (see Matthew 28:19-20 in the margin), in order to present every Christian complete or mature in Jesus. Paul wrote to the Colossians, "We proclaim him, admonishing and teaching everyone with all wisdom, so that we may present everyone perfect in Christ. To this end I labor, struggling with all his energy, which so powerfully works in me" (Colossians 1:28-29).

Therefore go and make disciples of all nations, baptizing them in the name of the Father and of the Son and of the Holy Spirit, and teaching them to obey everything I have commanded you. And surely I am with you always, to the very end of the age.
–Matthew 28:19-20

A leader cannot accomplish this overwhelming objective without keeping a heart for ministry. Scripture reminds us that spiritual transformation is the goal of the ministry of the church. Paul wrote, "And we, who with unveiled faces all reflect the Lord's glory, are being transformed into his likeness with ever-increasing glory, which comes from the Lord, who is the Spirit" (2 Corinthians 3:18).

Week 4, Day 1

WATCHING FOR SPIRITUAL TRANSFORMATION *continued . . .*

Notes

My friend Damon Shook is such a pastor. A colleague of mine who sat under his preaching for 14 years shared a very personal recollection. One day as he preached on God's never-ending desire and plan to break cycles of abuse and alcoholism, she was struck by the application to her own life. More than 50 years old at that time, she had been troubled all her life by the fact that her mother had left her as an 18-month-old infant. Her mother died many years later, a hopeless alcoholic. Growing up in the care of her father and an assortment of relatives, she had never understood how God could have allowed her to grow up without a mother. She later recounted how the knowledge that His intervention spared her the same fate as her mother had completely erased the bitter feelings over the loss of her mother! God used this caring, sensitive pastor in a miracle of transformation.

Today take some time to look at your heart. Remember that as a minister or leader, everything you do is about spiritual transformation, *first in you* and then in those to whom you minister.

Think about what you just read. Do you believe your life genuinely reflects someone who has been transformed spiritually? ❑ Yes ❑ No Below, write why you answered the way you did. If you checked yes, describe specific ways that you believe you demonstrate transformation.

____
____
____
____
____

Ask God to help you reveal a changed life to those to whom you minister. Ask Him to help you set as a goal the spiritual transformation of all the members in your church family.

Summary Points to Ponder

- Godly jealousy occurs when you have a heart for the church.
- Spiritual transformation is the goal of your ministry.
- Personal transformation in your own life is your top responsibility.

Week 4, Day 2

BROKEN-HEARTED LEADERSHIP

Earlier I mentioned how Brother Harvey, the experienced godly senior pastor with whom I worked in my first few years of ministry, was a role model for me. He taught me how to conduct funerals, visit hospitals, win souls to Christ, and preach. I will always be grateful to him for the personal investment he made in my life and ministry.

But the thing that really made Brother Harvey stand out was his brokenness in prayer. In the mornings, as I went down the hall to my office, I would hear him praying aloud. One day I stopped to listen — perhaps I shouldn't have eavesdropped, but I was curious. I heard Brother Harvey, with brokenness and tears, pray for the church and the many needs represented in the congregation.

From that experience I learned an essential lesson in leadership — that the best ministers lead with a broken heart. Without a broken heart, you cannot lead the church to accomplish the work God has given her to do.

Anguishing Over the Body
The apostle Paul illustrates the importance of leading God's people from the point of brokenness.

Read 2 Corinthians 2:4 in the margin. What was the purpose of Paul's tears?

____

Paul carried anguish in his heart over the condition of the Corinthian church. He cried over them because of His great love for them. He could have made excuses for members' actions. He could have moved on to other, more promising church situations. But he spent a great deal of time pouring out his heart over this troubled congregation.

Though the church included people who did not like Paul and who questioned his ministry, Paul did not allow these detractors to steal his heart for them and their spiritual growth. Too often I have put walls up in my own life to protect my heart rather than expose it to the attacks of some in the church.

This Week

For I wrote you out of great distress and anguish of heart and with many tears, not to grieve you but to let you know the depth of my love for you.
–2 Corinthians 2:4

Week 4, Day 2

BROKEN-HEARTED LEADERSHIP *continued . . .*

Notes

Like Paul, brokenhearted leaders love God's people regardless of their actions.

How do you respond when you encounter people who criticize you? Check any below that apply.

- ❑ Begin sending out my resumé and start looking for another place to serve. Or, if I'm a lay person, resign immediately from my committee, my Sunday School class, or my church role.
- ❑ Confront them angrily and blast them for how much they hurt me.
- ❑ Speak to them as diplomatically and courteously as I can and try to get to the root of the problem.
- ❑ Withdraw from them completely and freeze them out.
- ❑ Pray for them out of brokenness and love.
- ❑ Other ____
  ____

A Christian woman I know had ongoing difficulties relating to two relatives. When she left from visits with this husband and wife, she typically drove back to her home in tears, as she reflected on hurtful statements made during the visit. She grieved the fact that the relationship did not meet her expectations. Then one day, the Holy Spirit impressed on her the fact that these two relatives were unsaved and lost in sin. She changed her focus and determined that each time she visited, she would show Christ's love to them, regardless of what they said or did. Today, when she leaves their home after visiting, she still often cries, but her tears are for the empty spiritual condition of the couple, not for her own unmet needs. Her heart became broken not for herself but because of her great desire that these family members would come to know Christ in a personal relationship.

The Church in the Leader's Heart

The fact is that Paul had the church in his heart. He didn't separate himself from the church; he made the church his life. He writes to the Philippian church, "It is right for me to feel this way about all of you, since *I have you in my heart* [italics added]; for whether I am in chains or defending and confirming the gospel, all of you share in God's grace with me" (Philippians 1:7).

we made every effort to see you" (1 Thessalonians 2:17). He communicated to them, in effect, "I am away in presence, but my heart is present with you." The servant leader's heart stays with his people regardless of geography. Jesus said, "Where your treasure is, there your heart will be also" (Matthew 6:21). The leader keeps a heart for those he or she serves by maintaining good relationships with them.

What are some ways that you believe you work to maintain sound relationships with church members or with those you serve in your capacity as leader? Below, check any statements that apply.

- ❑ I try to be accessible to them, trying not to overschedule myself to the point that I have no time to see those who need my time.
- ❑ I try to practice good listening skills, so that I concentrate without distraction on each person as he or she talks to me.
- ❑ I work at maintaining good eye contact, so that I don't give the appearance that I'm looking around to speak to others when I'm involved in a one-on-one conversation.
- ❑ I pray for members' individual prayer requests, taking them to heart seriously and not making idle promises to remember their needs in prayer.
- ❑ I try to remember that these individuals — even those with whom I have difficulty — are people God has given me to shepherd and disciple. I seek His counsel in how to deal with difficult situations.
- ❑ I apologize quickly if I have wronged anyone and try to make amends.
- ❑ I guard my tongue and try to avoid making unkind remarks to or about anyone within the sphere of my ministry.
- ❑ Other ____

The Desire of the Leader's Heart

As you consider the wonder of relationships you enjoy with God's people, your desire must be unchanging. You want to see them mature in Christ. Paul said to the Colossians, "For though I am absent from you in body, I am present with you in spirit and delight to see how orderly you are and how firm your faith in Christ is" (Colossians 2:5).

Notes

Week 4, Day 3

THE POWER OF RELATIONSHIPS *continued . . .*

Notes

Paul longed in heart to see church members working in an orderly manner with each other while they maintained their steadfastness in Christ.

Frank is a deacon in Houston. He has been involved in his church's soul-winning efforts for a long time and has personally led countless people to Christ. Frank keeps a record of every new believer he has led to the Lord, and he can tell you today where they are and what they are doing. You see, he feels a sense of responsibility for them, and he wants to be sure that each person is maturing as a Christian.

How do you feel about the people you serve? When you keep your heart for the church, your heart remains with the people you serve.

One member, whose role in the church was to lead discipleship courses, rejoiced to see that each year after her class concluded, members consistently maintained contact with each other and fellowshipped together. Sometimes they invited her to group reunions; other times they linked up for dinner or other outings without their leader present. Rather than become petty or jealous when she happened on them together, this leader rejoiced that the people she had served were maturing in their relationships with each other and with Christ. Like Paul's reflection, this leader saw members of the body of Christ working in an orderly manner with each other while keeping Christ central.

Describe a scenario in your life that may resemble the vignettes I just told you about. Tell about a time when you experienced someone you served maturing in Christ, as an outgrowth of time you invested in this person.

____

____

____

____

____

____

____

____

Summary Points to Ponder

- A leader's heart remains with the church, regardless of where life leads.
- Keeping your heart for the church will strengthen relationships.
- The investment of your heart in another's life is an eternal investment.

Notes

Week 4, Day 4

NO COST TOO HIGH, NO SACRIFICE TOO GREAT

This Week

Day 1: Watching for Spiritual Transformation
Day 2: Broken-Hearted Leadership
Day 3: The Power of Relationships
Day 4: No Cost Too High, No Sacrifice Too Great
Day 5: Integrity of Heart and Skillfulness of Hands

A minister friend of mine has an unusual story. He grew up in and felt called to the ministry in the church where he now serves. First, he became the church's janitor. As people became drawn to him, the church asked him to serve as minister to youth. A few years later, he was called to be associate pastor there. Then, when the church's pastor retired, members turned to him to be their pastor. What a great relationship he has with this particular body of Christ!

A few years ago, my friend faced one of the greatest challenges in his ministry. A much larger, more high-profile church asked him if he would consider becoming their pastor. He was shocked that members there would think of him in this regard. He had always thought that if he ever left and served another church, it would be this particular one. It was the church he had always admired.

After much prayer seeking God's direction, he couldn't get the people of his current church out of his heart. He turned the larger church down and stayed with his people. He remained at a church with far fewer members at a much smaller salary. To a casual observer, it might appear that he made a large sacrifice, but he never looked back with regret. He said, "No sacrifice is too great for the people of this church."

For the minister who keeps his heart for the church, no cost is too great or sacrifice too high. Sacrificial leadership emerges from a heart for the church.

Make room for us in your hearts. We have wronged no one, we have corrupted no one, we have exploited no one. I do not say this to condemn you; I have said before that you have such a place in our hearts that we would live or die with you.
–2 Corinthians 7:2-3

Sacrificial Leadership
Paul spent much emotional energy on the Corinthian church. I have often thought that maybe he would have been better off just to go and plant a new church in Corinth rather than to put up with this troubled group of people! But Paul patiently ministered to the church in Corinth. His relationship with its people can only be explained as one of love.

Paul was willing to make great sacrifices for the church at Corinth. Read in the margin how he pleaded with them in 2 Corinthians 7:2-3.

In the Scripture you just read, underline the phrase that indicates the place the church had in Paul's heart.

Notes

In these verses, Paul openly calls the Corinthians to understand his heart for them. His heart is open to them. No cost is too high. He says he is even willing to die for them. Sacrifice epitomizes keeping a heart for the church.

In what ways do you sacrifice for the church? Check the following statements that apply, or supply your own.

- ❑ Guarding my tongue and watching statements I make that might cast aspersions on the body of Christ where I serve, even when "ventilating" to someone would make me feel better.
- ❑ Being discerning with my lifestyle, so that my material possessions reflect good stewardship of the funds God has entrusted to my care.
- ❑ Being available when people need me, even if that means I need to cancel a golf game or some other recreational outing to which I've looked forward.
- ❑ Turning down invitations to speak that would be flattering to my ego in order to stay close to those I serve in some critical time.
- ❑ Giving sacrificial time in prayer for members, even for those with whom I don't get along well.
- ❑ Other ______________________________

Wide Open Hearts

I am fascinated by Paul's willingness to open himself up to the Corinthians. Repeatedly he appeals to them to open themselves to his leadership as he opened himself to them. He writes, "We have spoken freely to you, Corinthians, and opened wide our hearts to you" (2 Corinthians 6:11).

Sometimes that openness can come across in the way you speak to your congregation, your class members, your committee members — those whom you serve. As you teach your Sunday School class, do you share with them how God has helped you in your struggles during the past week? As you relate to your committee, do you sacrifice a "know-it-all" attitude to be open to members' ideas and input? As you deliver a message or share a

Week 4, Day 4

NO COST TOO HIGH, NO SACRIFICE TOO GREAT *continued . . .*

Notes

devotional thought, do you tell how God has worked with you to overcome past pain or how you have repented to God for previous wrongdoing? Sacrifice can occur in those areas as well, when you are willing to show yourself as a fellow struggler. If you demonstrate to those you lead that God has worked through the difficulties in your life, you model for them a way to overcome bitterness and get a new take on their life circumstances. Keeping yourself open keeps your heart for ministry.

I want to have that kind of openhearted relationship with those to whom I minister. I desperately desire to have that kind of heart for the people God gives me to serve. The only way I can be like Paul is to keep my heart for the church. Because of Him, it's all for them — whatever the cost or the sacrifice!

Ask God to grant you that kind of openhearted relationship described. Ask Him to rid you of any fears you might have about openness. Jot down any specific hindrances you have discovered.

____

____

____

____

Summary Points to Ponder

- A heart for the church sacrifices for the good of God's people.
- A heart for the church is an open, loving heart.
- Only a heart of love will sacrifice for the church, no matter the cost.

Week 4, Day 5

INTEGRITY OF HEART AND SKILLFULNESS OF HANDS

At a retirement service for a minister friend, the chairman of deacons at the minister's church said something about him that I'll never forget. Countless tributes had already been paid to this retiring minister; guests honored him with remarks about how he had led people to Christ and ministered to hurting people.

However, the deacon chairman's words represented the highest tribute, in my estimation. The man testified, "For all these years our pastor has sacrificed for the church, but to me, the most outstanding thing about him is his integrity."

As a leader, shepherd God's people with integrity in your heart.

This Week

A Shepherd's Heart

Scripture describes the work of ministry as shepherding. In 1 Peter 5:2-3 in the margin, underline the words or phrases that indicate how ministers are to shepherd God's flock.

Be shepherds of God's flock that is under your care, serving as overseers—not because you must, but because you are willing, as God wants you to be; not greedy for money, but eager to serve; not lording it over those entrusted to you, but being examples to the flock.
—1 Peter 5:2-3

When you keep your heart for the church, you can minister willingly, eagerly, and by being an example, just as Peter directed in the passage you just read. As you watch your heart, you can begin to appreciate the pains and struggles of the people of God. Leadership with a shepherd's heart expresses itself in guiding the church (your class, your Christian school) willingly and lovingly.

Think about a time in your ministry when you believe you did the best job of serving willingly, eagerly, and by being an example. It may be your current area of service or one that occurred long ago. In the spaces below, describe that time and specify what tangible ways you demonstrated these qualities.

____

____

____

____

____

Week 4, Day 5

INTEGRITY OF HEART AND SKILLFULNESS OF HANDS *continued . . .*

"So he shepherded them according to the integrity of his heart, and guided them by the skillfulness of his hands."
–Psalm 78:72, NKJV

Integrity at the Forefront
The Bible describes David as the shepherd of the nation of Israel. In the Psalms you read two, specific characteristics of King David's leadership. **Note the verse in the margin and underline these characteristics.**

For the minister who has kept his heart for the church, a balance between integrity and skill occurs. Shepherding begins in the heart. You shepherd because you have a heart for the church. You guide its members with skillful hands. In my ministry, I try first to be sure that I have integrity of heart in my leadership of the church, not just skillfulness of my hands. Have you ever heard someone say of another person in the ministry, "Well, he's a good preacher, but he needs to be more of a pastor. He hardly speaks to me." Perhaps you've heard of a Sunday School teacher described this way: "She teaches excellent lessons, but she does poorly at one-on-one relationships." Or, of an outreach leader, "All she's interested in is having high numbers to turn in to the church office. When she goes on a church visitation, she starts pushing herself on the people and doesn't take time to get to know them." Or of some other church leader, "His walk doesn't match his talk. Outside of the church, his language is coarse, and he yells at his wife and kids." Each of those examples could reflect someone who employs great skill in a particular role but whose heart is deficient in integrity.

What are some other ways that you believe a skilled leader can demonstrate integrity of heart? Describe one here.

____
____
____
____
____
____
____

I hope you will reflect on the integrity of your own heart as reflected in your actions to shepherd or conduct the ministry that God has given to you. Integrity occurs as I keep my heart. When I keep my heart, I have a heart for the people of God to whom I minister. The same is true of you.

Stop and pray, asking God to help you know whether He's pleased with the degree of integrity He finds in your heart. Perhaps you may need to confess an incident when you depended more on your skill than on integrity of heart. Come clean before the Lord and ask for His help in serving with integrity. Remember, God's Holy Spirit stands ready to help in any area of weakness. He is your Advocate, Counselor, and Helper.

Notes

Summary Points to Ponder

- A heart for the church is expressed in a shepherd's heart.
- Integrity of heart is foundational to shepherding the church.
- Integrity of heart and skillfulness of hands are the shepherd's tools.
- When I keep my heart for the church, I will shepherd those under my care with integrity.

Notes

Week 5, Introduction

KEEPING YOUR HEART FOR THE WORLD

My wife and I lived in California during the time the devastating 1989 earthquake occurred in the Bay Area. During the 5:00 p.m. rush hour, a large portion of a freeway collapsed, trapping or killing hundreds of people. The World Series baseball game at Candlestick Park was stopped. Emergency personnel worked frantically to rescue any victims who might have survived the quake.

Several days later, a newspaper reporter located a young man who had worked with rescuers in the attempt to find survivors. He was dirty; his clothes were torn. When asked to comment on what he had seen and experienced during the past three days, he told several stories and concluded with the remark that, "All the sacrifice and effort was worth it if we found just one person alive!"

This week you will focus on keeping your heart for the world. God has sent you on a rescue mission. All your efforts and sacrifices are worth it if just one person comes to know Christ. A commitment to be a soul-winner requires a heart for those who are lost and without Christ. Use these days to evaluate your heart and your passion for seeing the world come to know Him as Savior and Lord.

This Week

Day 1: The Pain that Never Goes Away
Day 2: A Great Desire
Day 3: A Love that Compels
Day 4: Seeing the World as Jesus Does
Day 5: A Heart Like His

Week 5, Day 1

THE PAIN THAT NEVER GOES AWAY

This Week

For Christ's love compels us, because we are convinced that one died for all, and therefore all died . . . . All this is from God, who reconciled us to himself through Christ and gave us the ministry of reconciliation.
–2 Corinthians 5:14, 18

O Jerusalem, Jerusalem, you who kill the prophets and stone those sent to you, how often I have longed to gather your children together, as a hen gathers her chicks under her wings, but you were not willing.
–Matthew 23:37

A woman was passionately involved with a group that assisted teenagers who were addicted to drugs. She spent her own money and time to help these troubled teens.

When someone asked her why she gave herself so wholeheartedly to such a difficult ministry, the woman gave this reply. "When my daughter died from a drug overdose, I thought I would never get over it. I tried to avoid other people; I was ashamed of my daughter's actions and the shame it brought to our family. Finally, I determined that the best way for me to deal with my feelings was to do something to help other teenagers trapped in drug abuse. A pain in my heart that never goes away keeps me working with these kids."

A pain that never goes away describes what is in your heart as you seek to carry out the work that the Lord gave to you in the world. Yours is a mission of reconciliation (2 Corinthians 5:14, 18). God has called you to minister in order that every person might hear and receive the good news that Jesus Christ can make a difference in their lives.

Jesus had a pain for the world that never went away (see Matthew 23:37 in the margin). Matthew describes how He wept over Jerusalem. His heart was broken over the lostness of the world. He saw the people as sheep without a shepherd. He had the world on His heart.

In what way do you have the world on your heart? Perhaps you have watched a TV newscast or read a newspaper report about a disaster occurring in a foreign country and genuinely grieved as you realized that vast numbers of unsaved people must have perished in that disaster. Describe your experience here. ______________________________

____

____

____

Grief for Hard-Hearted People

The gospel writers provide some insight into how Jesus reacted to the hard-heartedness of the people as He went about doing His work. On one occasion

He entered the synagogue and saw a man with a withered hand. It was the Sabbath. He determined to heal the man. Mark writes, "He looked around at them in anger and, deeply distressed at their stubborn hearts, said to the man, 'Stretch out your hand'"(Mark 3:5).

I often think about this story and apply it to my own life in ministry. At times I am guilty of doing my work with a hard heart. My ministry can be formal, cold, and predictable. Yet I am challenged by the example of the Lord Jesus, who always carried out His ministry with a heart for those trapped in bondage to sin.

Jesus went through all the towns and villages, teaching in their synagogues, preaching the good news of the kingdom and healing every disease and sickness. When he saw the crowds, he had compassion on them, because they were harassed and helpless, like sheep without a shepherd.
–Matthew 9:35-36

Jesus' heart was broken for those who were in bondage to sin, sickness, and disease. He was grieved over those religious leaders who had hard hearts. See the verses at right.

In what ways do you find yourself guilty of performing your ministry with a heart that is hardened to the plight of all who are lost? Below check any descriptions that apply.

- ❑ Going through the motions of sermon preparation without asking God to give me His words and His inspiration that would inspire members to grieve for the lost
- ❑ Preaching "easy messages" that will make my members feel good instead of messages that will challenge them to have a heart for the world
- ❑ Allowing bitterness over some past slight to keep me from supporting wholeheartedly a committee recommendation or a new program that might open members' eyes to the lost of our community and our world
- ❑ Failing to take care of myself physically and emotionally, allowing burnout to creep in and thus harden my heart for the Lord's work and for the world
- ❑ Feeling hopeless and helpless — believing that nothing I do could make much difference anyway about those who are lost
- ❑ Believing that those I serve (my class, committee, prayer group, congregation) are needy enough as it is without adding concerns about lost people outside my church
- ❑ Allowing haughtiness and pride, which keep me self-satisfied with my church's growth or programs, to prevent me from recognizing the

Week 5, Day 1

THE PAIN THAT NEVER GOES AWAY *continued . . .*

spiritually needy all around me and the lost and dying in darkened nations of the world

❑ Other ____

Continual Sorrow in the Heart

When you keep the world on your heart, you will always experience a pain that never goes away. No matter where you look, suffering and trouble exist. The brokenness of people's lives can be overwhelming. But your ministry is at its best when you carry that pain in your heart. Jesus was a man of sorrows and acquainted with grief.

The Apostle Paul also carried a pain in his heart that would not go away.

I speak the truth in Christ – I am not lying, my conscience confirms it in the Holy Spirit – I have great sorrow and unceasing anguish in my heart. For I could wish that I myself were cursed and cut off from Christ for the sake of my brothers, those of my own race, the people of Israel.
–Romans 9:1-3

Read Romans 9:1-3 at left. For whom did Paul carry this great pain?

____

Paul vividly described the pain of having the lost on your heart as you do ministry. He had great sorrow and continued grief. He wished that he could be accursed for his countrymen – his fellow Jews. He had a pain for the lost.

I don't like pain in my life. In every way that I can, I try to avoid it or get rid of it. Yet a pain exists in my heart that I never want to lose — the pain of feeling and recognizing the lostness of the world. Keeping your heart for the world requires that you carry a pain for people without Christ.

Stop and pray. Ask God to forgive you for the times you have been insensitive to the lostness of others. Ask Him to help you stay aware of the people around you, both nearby and far away, who need Him. Instead of praying silently or aloud, do something different this time. Below, write out your thoughts in a prayer to God.

____

____

____

____

____

Summary Points to Ponder

- When you keep your heart for the world, you will grieve over the lost.
- When you keep your heart for the world, the pain for the lost never goes away.
- When you keep your heart for the world, that same pain motivates you in your ministry.
- When you keep your heart for the world, you never lose your heart for ministry.

Notes

Week 5, Day 2

A GREAT DESIRE

This Week

My friend Bobby is a singularly focused individual. He is consumed with a passion to win people to Christ. Regardless of who you are or where you are from, Bobby wants to be sure that you have heard about Christ and how He can change your life.

When Bobby was in the Vietnam war, he was critically wounded. His life flashed before him. He thought he would certainly die. On his way to the hospital, he asked God to spare his life. He reported realizing that he had not lived for the Lord as he should. He renewed his commitment to Christ. He determined that for the rest of his life, he would be a witness for Christ. He has done so through the years. He has a consuming desire to see people saved, and God has honored and blessed his life.

Bobby's example challenges me to the same singular desire — to see people come to know Christ. That is what keeping your heart for the world means. Keeping the world on your heart pushes you to have a passion to reach people with the gospel.

Brothers, my heart's desire and prayer to God for the Israelites is that they may be saved.
–Romans 10:1

The Rudder that Steers the Ship

When Paul described his heart's desire for Israel, he expressed the essence of keeping the world on your heart in ministry in the verse at left. Paul's heart's desire was for the salvation of Israel. As I keep my heart for the world, I find myself constantly evaluating my desires. What is it that I desire in ministry: fame, recognition, appreciation, prestige, or comfort? Paul set the example for you and me. It is one of focusing the heart on seeing people come to know Christ as Savior and Lord.

Reread this last paragraph. Ask yourself the question posed there: What do I desire most in my ministry: fame? recognition? appreciation? prestige? comfort? the desire of seeing people to know Christ as Savior? You don't have to write out your answer to this question. This time, your answer is between you and God. If you weren't able to answer that the singular passion of your life is the same as is my friend Bobby's, what would it take for you to have this as your passion? Stop and pray about this matter before you go further in today's work.

A prominent pastor was considered to be one of the finest preachers ever graduated from his seminary. He and his wife bought a fine home in the lovely subdivision surrounding their church. They entertained church people constantly. The pastor's name was mentioned frequently as the leading candidate for the presidency of his denomination. Everything looked promising for this diligent pastor. However, under the surface, ego and vanity were the rudders steering the ship in this man's life. The fame, recognition, and comfort that he enjoyed represented the passion of his life rather than the desire to see people come to know Christ as Savior. After a few years, this pastor resigned from his pulpit and decided to pursue a job in another field.

In contrast, consider the story of a young marine and his family.

> Our military family has served as non-traditional missionaries for the past fifteen years. We've served God and country through Southern Baptist churches in each of the four civilian communities in which we lived. After marriage, my wife and I were members of a large, vital and growing church. Over a four-year period, we had the privilege of starting two new adult classes while learning how to effectively minister to military families through the Sunday School. That church focused on loving God and making disciples. The leadership had a vision and the church bought into that vision.
>
> Though I had been a Christian nearly all of my life, I had rarely experienced the dynamic influence of a committed local church that I experienced there. It became the standard by which we measured every other church that followed.
>
> At our next duty station, we felt God's call to put that good training to use in a church that really needed trained laymen. Although we used the same methods we had previously learned, we saw no growth in our class or church, and became frustrated. We felt defeated. When we received orders to move halfway around the world, we left bowed but not broken. Our church was preoccupied with its history, proud of a tradition going back to the early 1800's. But there was no vision — future or present. Now, six years later, that church is still struggling to find a vision, a mission and predictably, a pastor.

Notes

Week 5, Day 2

A GREAT DESIRE *continued . . .*

Notes

We visited seven churches before hearing God's call to a new church home. There, we were in the minority, both racially and vocationally, but we have not been in a more accepting or loving church before or since. This church was missions-minded, giving time, money, talents, and even vacations to missions. Staying on mission was easy for us, and we were genuinely sorry to leave.

Upon our return to the same area as our second church, we felt God's call to a church nearer the base where we live and work, a place that in spiritual terms was (and is) a real fixer-upper! "FBC Status Quo" has been flat-lined in growth for nearly thirty years with no vision, no detectable mission, and no plans for growth beyond a family life center. Thousands of servicemen and their families move in and out of this church's shadow every year, and yet there has never been a vision or plan to reach the lost and unchurched for Christ.

Many times we have felt like cutting our losses and moving our membership. We've been tempted to pray for orders to a new duty station. We've wondered if the community would be better served if this church died. Is no witness better than a bad one? And soon we began to focus on us, rather than Him. Are we wasting "our" time, "our" money, "our" talents, "our" this and "our" that? Suddenly, it was about us.

Such thoughts distracted us from our mission — to love God and make disciples. Though the circumstances are not to our liking, they are the ones God called us to. The mission here is no different than in that first church that we mistakenly label as the ideal. Truth is, that church had problems too; we've just conveniently forgotten them. What has kept us here with our hands firmly on the plow is the memory of God's unmistakable call. We are here not by accident, but by His calling. We aren't here to complain about what's wrong or to whine about some "better" church in our past. And, it's not about us. Our job is to love God and get about the business of making disciples, right here, right now. And that keeps us going!

Keeping your heart for the world involves constant introspection, asking yourself, "What is the rudder that steers my ship in ministry?" If the answer is anything other than a heart for the world, get down on your knees and confess this to God. Ask Him to give you a desire to keep your heart for the ministry.

The Bible says that God will give you the desire of your heart. I often think that when I desire to see others come to Christ, I am most "at one" with God.

In 2 Peter 3:9, at right, underline what Peter describes as being the Lord's great desire.

The Lord is not slow in keeping his promise, as some understand slowness. He is patient with you, not wanting anyone to perish, but everyone to come to repentance.
–2 Peter 3:9

God's desire is that all people might come to repentance and be saved. When I keep my heart for the world, I share His passion. Pray that God will help you shape your ministry around this great desire.

Think about a time in your ministry when you feel you most had this desire — that all people be saved — at the forefront of all your activities. Perhaps it is the current period in which you are ministering. For some it might have been during their first pastorate, when they first became a deacon, or at some other time. After you get this time fixed in your mind, try to remember what this period was like for you and what you did to demonstrate this focus. *(Example: I had just completed an intensive discipleship course. I began recognizing the lost condition of many people I encountered. Whenever possible, I tried to speak to them about Christ.)*

____

____

____

____

Perhaps the Lord is calling you to do more than just recognize and be aware of those who are lost. Perhaps you are being stirred to take some concrete action in your city, state, or in some other corner of the world. Read the list below. Check any items that you are doing or would consider doing to bring others to Christ.

- ❑ Develop a new outreach initiative in my church
- ❑ Give sacrificially to spread the gospel

Week 5, Day 2

A GREAT DESIRE *continued . . .*

Notes

- ❑ Pray daily for missionaries who serve in my country and in countries around the world
- ❑ Consider giving my time, either as a volunteer at home or in a short-term program overseas
- ❑ Help my church adopt an unreached people group for whom we can pray
- ❑ Consider going myself or sending volunteers to prayerwalk in areas where many are unsaved (perhaps on the street where you live)
- ❑ Contact the local or state offices of my denomination to find out about missions projects I can lead my church or group to support
- ❑ Consider whether the Lord might be calling me to serve Him as a career missionary, transplanting my life into another culture for the purpose of bringing others to Christ
- ❑ Other ____
____

As you conclude this day's work with prayer, ask God to give you courage to take bold steps to help people be saved — perhaps even to give you boldness to take one of the steps you checked in the previous exercise.

Summary Points to Ponder

- When you keep your heart for the world, you will desire for people to come to know Christ in a personal relationship.
- When you keep your heart for the world, your desire for people to be saved will become the rudder that steers the ship of your ministry.
- When you keep your heart for the world, you will have a growing passion for the lost.
- When you keep your heart for the world, you share God's desire for all people.

Notes

Week 5, Day 3

A LOVE THAT COMPELS

This Week

My deacon friend Delbert has a unique ministry that I have always appreciated. Through the years he has developed a relationship with the local sheriff's department. When men are released from jail, Delbert invites them to his home. He has converted his garage into a clothing store, where he has collected clothes of all sizes, along with shoes and boots.

When a man is released from prison, he can visit Delbert's garage and pick out clothing to help him get started in his new life. Then Delbert arranges to bring him to church on Sunday or help him get a bus ticket home.

Once our church went to the rescue mission to conduct weekly services. I began looking for Delbert and couldn't find him. Finally, I located him in the back entrance, cutting the hair of the men who needed haircuts. While he cut their hair, he shared the gospel with them. When asked why he performs this work, Delbert tells others, "The love of God pushes me." When you keep your heart for ministry, the love of God will push you out into the world.

Accountability in Ministry
Second Corinthians 5 is one of the greatest sections in all the Bible in describing a Christian's responsibility to the world. Here Paul expresses clearly the reasons he was so passionate about reaching people for Christ.

For we must all appear before the judgment seat of Christ, so that each one may receive what is due him for the things done while in the body, whether good or bad.
—2 Corinthians 5:10

Read 2 Corinthians 5:10 in the margin. Answer the following questions, as they apply to you:
For what person's ministry am I accountable? ______________________
For whom will I have to answer someday when I stand before Christ?
____
What will happen when Christ judges me? ______________________

Paul reminds you that you are accountable for the work God has given you to do. He further states that one day you will stand before the Judgment Seat of Christ to give an account for your work. He will determine what is due you for how well or how poorly you have carried out the ministry of reconciliation that God has given to you. I take this verse from 2 Corinthians very seriously, because it doesn't mince words in telling me what is ahead for me. I try to avoid being distracted by less important things so I can be prepared for that day.

Was there ever a time when you tried to slack off in your ministry because you believed you were already doing far more than others on your church staff, or others against whom you compared yourself? If so, describe that time here.

____
____
____
____
____
____

Peter turned and saw that the disciple whom Jesus loved was following them . . . . When Peter saw him, he asked, "Lord, what about him?" Jesus answered, "If I want him to remain alive until I return, what is that to you? You must follow me."
–John 21:20-21

The interaction between Peter and Jesus, depicted in John 21 at right, shows very clearly what Jesus thinks of our tendency to become overly concerned with someone else's actions, or the lack thereof. On the great judgement day, you won't have to answer for how well another Christian has lived life on earth. It will be your case and your case alone that is reviewed when you stand before Christ. Jesus' command to Peter was, "You must follow me." This is your mandate from Christ as well.

The Terror of the Lord and Persuading Men

When you keep your heart for the world, you remember that the time is short in which you can carry out your ministry.

Since, then, we know what it is to fear the Lord, we try to persuade men. What we are is plain to God, and I hope it is also plain to your conscience.
–2 Corinthians 5:11

Read 2 Corinthians 5:11 in the margin. Then mark the following statements about Paul T (if true) or F (if false.)

____ Paul preached about Christ because he feared what the disciples would think of him if he didn't.
____ Paul realized he could continue to deceive the Lord if he failed to preach the gospel.
____ Paul performed his ministry out of a desire to bolster his own ego.
____ Paul persuaded others to follow Christ because he feared the Lord.

Week 5, Day 3

A LOVE THAT COMPELS *continued . . .*

Notes

Paul reveals that he persuaded people to be saved because of the terror of the Lord. He knew the day of judgment was coming. Because of the fear of that awful judgment, his heart was ignited with a passion to reach people for Christ. Paul persuaded others because he feared God, who could not be deceived about his actions. He did not tell about Jesus to bolster others' opinions of him or because he had a big ego. The fear of the Lord that brings reverence and awe into your life is an important motive in seeking to persuade others to become Christians. (I'm sure you saw that the last statement in the above exercise is the only one that is true.)

The Love of Christ Pushes You

Perhaps the most significant way you can rekindle your passion for the lost is through the love of Christ. You can have the same motivation as my friend Delbert: the love of Christ can push you. Paul said it like this, "For Christ's love compels us, because we are convinced that one died for all, and therefore all died. And he died for all, that those who live should no longer live for themselves" (2 Corinthians 5:14-15).

One Christian laywoman described a time when she felt that Christ's love literally pushed her into ministry: "I was parking my car at the post office when I noticed a vehicle stalled in another portion of the parking lot. The stalled car was blocking traffic. An elderly woman stood outside the car, looking panicked. Although I was rushing to get back to my office, I felt the Holy Spirit moving me to assist the woman. I asked her if I could help. She seemed grateful that someone had stopped to notice her plight. She asked if I could call her supervisor and explain that she would be late and also call the mechanic who usually works on her car. I flagged down two other post office customers to push the car away from traffic. I insisted that the woman wait inside the post office out of the heat. I drove to my business, a few minutes away, and made the calls as she requested. Then I returned to report to the woman that help was on the way. She thanked me profusely and offered to pay me for my sacrifice of time. I replied that no payment was necessary and said that I had done what I had because of the love of Christ in my heart. She replied, 'Thank you for showing love to an old Jewish lady.' I was thankful that Christ's love nudged me beyond my comfort zone so that I had no choice but to help."

Describe a time when the love of Christ literally pushed you into some act of ministry.

____
____
____
____

The love of Christ in your heart pushes you into the world. The love of Christ helps you sacrifice selfish desires and take up the cause of Christ. When I consider the great love of Christ for me, it warms my heart. I want to share His love with others. I am pushed into the world by the love of Christ!

In prayer, ask the Father to strategically shove you in the areas where He needs you to minister.

Summary Points to Ponder

- When you keep your heart for the world, you are accountable for your ministry.
- When you keep your heart for the world, you are stirred by the coming judgment of God.
- When you keep your heart for the world, you are renewed by Christ's love.
- When you keep your heart for the world, you sacrifice for the sake of the world.

Notes

Week 5, Day 4

SEEING THE WORLD AS JESUS DOES

This Week

A pastor of a very large church regularly challenged a friend of mine who served on his staff. After a staff meeting, this pastor typically would call my friend aside and say to him, "Bill, don't you see it? Don't you see it?" The pastor believed Bill had the unique ability to look beyond the current situations of life and recognize the hand of God at work in a situation or a circumstance.

I have often thought about those words from that pastor. In seeking to keep my heart for the world, I have often not seen things from God's perspective. I have been blind to the work that God was doing through what appeared to be a series of terrible events.

At times I find myself consumed with anger by the way that people live. I forget to look at them with spiritual eyes. When I keep my perspective on the world as Jesus did, I begin to see things His way. Today you have an opportunity to check out your heart against the Lord Jesus and against His heart for the world. He saw the world differently than most people who ministered in His time. He can teach you the way to see from the heart.

He Saw and Was Moved

When Jesus ministered among the multitudes, it was from the heart. He had the world on His heart. It showed in His actions. His words were full of love for those lost in their sin and those in desperate circumstances.

When he saw the crowds, he had compassion on them, because they were harassed and helpless, like sheep without a shepherd.
–Matthew 9:36

Read the passage appearing in the margin. Underline the phrase that indicates how Jesus reacted when He saw the multitudes.

Jesus saw the crowds and was moved with compassion. Jesus' eyes were connected to His heart. What do you see as you minister? Is your heart moved? Are you touched by what you see in the world? When you read about someone being arrested for a crime in your community, are you filled with loathing for the accused, or do you think, "That person probably doesn't know Jesus as Savior and is lost in sin"? When you hear about an elected official being involved in a scandal, do you stop and pray for the condition of that person's soul?

Think about those questions for just a moment. Let your mind drift to a situation in which you looked with compassion on someone who was under siege or in trouble and describe it here.

____
____
____
____
____

Notes

I'm reminded about a story involving a young man in trouble and the response of his Quaker church family. The young man had stolen a car and had been caught red-handed. The elders of his church met, and the serious situation was presented by one of the men. Their immediate response was, "Where did we go wrong? How have we failed this boy, allowing him to get into this kind of trouble?" Their first thoughts were not of blame, criticism, or even punishment. Because they loved him and were concerned about him spiritually, they demonstrated compassion for him in his crisis.

When Jesus looked on the multitudes, He saw them lacking a shepherd. They needed someone to care for them, to guide them, to protect them. Today in your ministry, people are in the same condition. When you keep your heart for the world, you can reach out and minister to a helpless world with a heart of compassion.

Under what type of situations do you see sheep lacking a shepherd? Below check any of the statements that apply, or name one of your own.

- ❑ People who have no moral standards, living together without benefit of marriage
- ❑ Individuals who are governed by the world's standards about possessions, spending well beyond their ability to pay
- ❑ Families that are so consumed with spending their time in recreational activities that they fail to observe the Lord's Day in a house of worship
- ❑ People who have never heard the good news of the gospel — helpless and hopeless
- ❑ Christians who are bound up in a "works" mentality and who fail to recognize the role of grace in the forgiveness of sin

Week 5, Day 4

SEEING THE WORLD AS JESUS DOES

continued . . .

Notes

- ❑ People whose total identity lies in their jobs and who fail to set aside time for family or church
- ❑ Other ____
____

Describe a ministry that you have had (or that you could have) with one of the groups that you checked or the one about which you wrote. *(Example: Instead of looking judgmentally on the homeless people who camp out around our church, we began Sunday School classes for their children.)*

____

____

____

____

Whenever Jesus saw and was moved by the crowds, He always responded in ministry to them. The same is true when you keep your heart for the world. You see, you are moved, and you minister!

As you pray to conclude today's work, ask the Father to give you Jesus' heart of compassion for people around you, especially those who are in a desperate condition.

Summary Points to Ponder

- When I keep my heart for the world, I see the desperate condition of the lost.
- When I keep my heart for the world, my heart is moved with love.
- When I keep my heart for the world, I minister out of love.

Week 5, Day 5

A HEART LIKE HIS

An older minister who prayed in a meeting I attended voiced some words in his prayer that stirred and challenged me. He prayed, "O God, don't give me fame, fortune, or recognition. Just give me a heart like Jesus." I left that prayer meeting thinking, "Wow, what a prayer! All that man of God asked was to have a heart like Jesus." I had heard and preached sermons on David, the man after God's own heart. But seldom had I thought much about the heart of Jesus and how important it is to have His heart.

Today, as you close this study on keeping your heart for ministry, consider Jesus as the model for a minister's heart. Pause today to be awed by the Lord Jesus' wonderful grace and kindness as He ministered to a world of hateful and broken people.

Driven by Love
Several times in Matthew's gospel you read about the compassion of Jesus. On one occasion, the Lord expressed concern for a tired and hungry crowd of people. His concern extended from their spiritual condition to their physical state. See the verse in the margin.

Here is a glimpse into the heart of the Lord Jesus. Out of a heart of compassion He ministered to the people. The heart of Jesus is a heart of ministry driven by love. At the heart of your ministry is love — love for the unlovely, the hateful, the rude, the arrogant, and the broken. When you keep your heart for the world, you minister out of love. Jesus' ministry was a ministry of the heart.

Think about the types of people mentioned in the paragraph you just read. They are listed again below. Stop and think about one person who fits each description. You may want to write that person's initials by the side of the adjective. The most important thing is that you make a concrete application to what you just read.

the unlovely ________________
the hateful ________________
the rude ________________
the arrogant ________________
the broken ________________

This Week

Jesus called his disciples to him and said, "I have compassion for these people; they have already been with me three days and have nothing to eat. I do not want to send them away hungry, or they may collapse on the way."
–Matthew 15:32

Week 5, Day 5

A HEART LIKE HIS *continued . . .*

Notes

For example, when you read the description, "the unlovely," you may think about the church member who wrote you a highly critical note about one of your sermons. For "the hateful," you may recall the person who bitterly challenged you in a church business meeting. For "the rude," you may think about the irregular attender in your Sunday school class who rebuffed you when you stopped by her house on an outreach visit. For "the arrogant," you may think about the member of the prayer group you lead who consistently tries to take over the meeting time and monopolize the discussion. When you think about "the broken," you may remember the youth who painfully confided in you last week that she has an unplanned pregnancy and is considering how to deal with her dilemma.

The people who come to your mind may be totally different than the examples I've suggested above. Regardless of the circumstance, Jesus has a heart for individuals in these categories. While He lived as a man, He had a heart ministry to others, regardless of how they treated Him or attempted to thwart Him.

A struggling, new congregation met in a day-care center while members considered where to locate permanently. The manager of the day-care center resented the church people and constantly complained about their lack of care of the building, even though her concerns could not be documented. Finally she called the pastor and ordered the church to move out. On the church's last Sunday in the center, the pastor asked the center manager to attend the morning worship service. During the service, he effusively thanked her for providing the space for the church during the months it had met there. He had a special plaque made to honor her, offered a donation to the center, and led a prayer asking the Lord to continue to bless her and her business. Instead of responding angrily about being evicted, the pastor surrounded the complaining woman with kindness. He operated with a heart like Jesus.

Describe a time when you have responded in a situation like this pastor did — surrounding an "unlovely" person with kindness despite mistreatment of you. ______________________________

____

____

Poured Out into the Heart
In our Lord's ministry, He faced many distractions and obstacles, just as you do. He was misunderstood, despised, and rejected. However, His love for the world guarded His heart. From a heart full of love, He came to the world. When He prayed that powerful prayer just before the crucifixion, He said, "I have made you known to them, and will continue to make you known in order that the love you have for me may be in them and that I myself may be in them" (John 17:26).

Let your ministry come from a heart guarded by the love of God, just as Jesus' was. Paul said, in Romans 5:5, "And hope does not disappoint us, because God has poured out his love into our hearts by the Holy Spirit, whom he has given us." I can keep my heart since the love of God has been poured out in my heart by the Holy Spirit. Out of that love for God and the world, I do my ministry. I challenge you to do likewise!

Summary Points to Ponder

- A heart like Jesus is a heart of love for the lost.
- A heart like Jesus causes me to minister to the hurting and lost.
- A heart like Jesus is guarded by the love of God in my heart.
- My highest aspiration must be to have a heart like Jesus.

To bring your study to a close, go back and scan through the pages of your workbook. In the blanks below, write down one key thought or concept that you most remember or found most helpful from each week's work.

Week 1: Your Heart, Your Ministry

____

____

Week 2: Keeping Your Heart for God

____

____

Notes

Week 5, Day 5

A HEART LIKE HIS *continued . . .*

Notes

Week 3: Keeping Your Heart for the Kingdom

Week 4: Keeping Your Heart for the Church

Week 5 : Keeping Your Heart for the World

Now write at least one commitment about keeping your heart for the ministry you have made while you have been involved in this study.

Close your study with prayer, asking God to help you keep the commitment you've just described. Invite His Holy Spirit to guide you day by day in keeping your heart for ministry.

Congratulations on completing this study of *Keeping Your Heart for Ministry.* I pray God will use what you've learned and applied to strengthen your work in His kingdom. Take a moment to read the "Final Thoughts" expressed on the next few pages.

Final Thoughts . . .

KEEPING YOUR HEART FOR MINISTRY

As I wrote this book, I prayed that you might pause and take the time to determine if you have lost your heart for ministry. Perhaps you have recognized some pitfalls or tendencies that could cause you to lose your heart. In the study, you have read many examples from Scripture, and I have shared my own personal struggles to keep my heart in ministry.

I wanted to close our time together with the testimony of a man in scripture who more than any other helps us keep our perspective on this important issue. That man is the apostle Paul. Perhaps no letter Paul penned expresses more of his personal feelings than the book of 2 Corinthians. In this book, Paul shares many insights into his own passions for ministry. He openly and transparently tells the Corinthian church about his spiritual struggles, yet he testifies to the church that he does his ministry without losing heart.

Let me summarize several insights that may help and encourage you.

Paul reminds us that God gives us our ministry, and that God makes us sufficient for ministry (See 2 Corinthians 3:6 at right). He also declares that the Holy Spirit empowers us in ministry In this verse He calls, He declares Himself our sufficiency, and He empowers! Just think of it! The wonderful ministry you and I are called to carry out for the Lord is given with assurance that the Holy Spirit will equip and empower us to do the work.

He has made us competent as ministers of a new covenant – not of the letter but of the Spirit: for the letter kills, but the Spirit gives life.
–2 Corinthians 3:6

Paul describes the ministry we've been given as eternal in the verses at right (2 Corinthians 4:17-18). Whether or not our ministries are appreciated during our lifetime, they carry eternal consequences and rewards. The things we do for Christ now will be rewarded someday in heaven!

For our light and momentary troubles are achieving for us an eternal glory that far outweighs them all. So we fix our eyes not on what is seen, but on what is unseen. For what is seen is temporary, but what is unseen is eternal.
–2 Corinthians 4:17-18

Paul then goes on to develop another very important theme. He tells the Corinthian church that we don't have to lose heart in ministry. In 2 Corinthians 4, Paul describes five essential principles that will keep us from losing our heart in ministry.

First, when we renounce the hidden things of shame (see v. 2 in the margin on the next page), we won't lose heart. Like Solomon, our hearts are often captured by people, causes, or things. Only when we renounce these idols and secret sins can we maintain real heart in ministry.

Final Thoughts . . .

KEEPING YOUR HEART FOR MINISTRY *continued . . .*

Rather, we have renounced secret and shameful ways; we do not use deception, nor do we distort the word of God. On the contrary, by setting forth the truth plainly we commend ourselves to every man's conscience in the sight of God.
–2 Corinthians 4:2

But we have this treasure in jars of clay to show that this all-surpassing power is from God and not from us.
–2 Corinthians 4:7

For our light and momentary troubles are achieving for us an eternal glory that far outweighs them all. So we fix our eyes not on what is seen, but on what is unseen. For what is seen is temporary, but what is unseen is eternal.
–2 Corinthians 4:17-18

Second, when we speak truthfully in our ministry (v. 2), we don't lose heart. Truth and integrity protect our hearts, guarding against falsehood and deceitfulness. We must always remember that ministry must be done in truthfulness and integrity.

Third, when we remember that we do our ministry in the frailty of our human condition; (v. 7), we don't lose heart. We aren't superhuman. We don't lose heart when we pace ourselves in ministry. When we keep our focus on the fact that we do our ministry out of clay pots, that is the idea of this passage.

Fourth, when we rely on God's power in ministry (v. 7), we don't lose heart. Jesus said in John 15:5 "apart from me you can do nothing." We cannot do our God-called ministry in our own strength; we must have God's power to do God's ministry.

Fifth, when we walk by faith, looking at the unseen, we don't lose heart. Paul understood the unseen in his ministry (vs. 17-18). He walked by faith, not by sight. When things looked hopeless, when he lay bleeding after being beaten, when he sat in a damp, dark dungeon as a consequence of his ministry, he didn't lose heart, because he saw the unseen. He knew the call of God to be certain in his life, and he trusted that what he did for God would have eternal consequences. He didn't lose heart.

And you, friend, what about you? Likely you have experienced some of the same difficulties as those I've shared with you throughout *Keeping Your Heart for Ministry*. Perhaps you've read a passage or verse that encourages you to press on. Make no mistake. The dangers, the pitfalls, the opportunities to lose heart are there. But One Who is greater than all stands ready to help. His Word is your personal guide. His Holy Spirit is your Helper and Advocate. He promises to empower you. Don't lose heart!

Michael D. Miller

KEEPING YOUR HEART FOR MINISTRY COVENANT

As you participate in ***Keeping Your Heart for Ministry***, you are asked to dedicate yourself to God and to your ***Keeping Your Heart for Ministry*** small group by making several commitments. Right now, you may not be able to do everything listed, but by signing this covenant, you pledge to adopt these practices as you progress through the study.

As a disciple of Jesus Christ, I commit myself to —

- Acknowledge Jesus Christ as Lord of my life each day.
- Attend all group sessions unless providentially hindered.
- Spend the time necessary to complete my daily assignments.
- Have a daily quiet time.
- Love and encourage each member of my group.
- Keep in strict confidence anything shared by others in the group sessions.
- Willingly submit myself to others in matters of accountability.
- Pray daily for group members.

Your small-group members will sign in the space provided to pledge their commitment to this Covenant. Pray for them daily.

____________________________ ____________________________

____________________________ ____________________________

____________________________ ____________________________

____________________________ ____________________________

____________________________ ____________________________

Signed:________________________ Date:________________________

Leader Guide

Introduction

LEADER GUIDE

Notes

K*eeping Your Heart for Ministry* offers exciting opportunities to assemble small group sessions for a deep, meaningful Bible study and for the personal application of principles presented in the study. This *Leader Guide* outlines a step-by-step method for facilitating small-group sessions for each of the five weeks of study.

The Process of *Keeping Your Heart for Ministry*

The *Keeping Your Heart for Ministry* study employs an interactive learning process. Each day for five days a week, members are expected to study a segment of the material and complete activities that relate to what they just read. Each day's work requires 20 to 30 minutes of study time.

At the end of the week's study, members gather for group sessions. The sessions help members reflect on the concepts and experiences in *Keeping Your Heart for Ministry* and apply the ideas to their lives.

Although persons may benefit from completing the studies totally on their own, without a group experience, they will have missed the critical element Jesus' disciples experienced: relationships with one another in Christ's presence. As members share their own testimonies about growing in wholehearted ministry, others give feedback and are encouraged in their own challenges and victories. Therefore, individuals are highly urged to connect with others within the body of Christ to study this material.

The small group study process creates a learning atmosphere that:
- promotes the sharing of common experiences;
- provides accountability for participants seeking life-change; and
- recreates the type of learning experiences Jesus used with His disciples.

Notes

Who Should Participate in a Small-Group Study?

This leadership resource would work well for a group of pastors, staff members, Christian schoolteachers, Christian school administrators, or denominational leaders. Ministry leaders — women's, men's, youth, or Bible study, for example — will find particular help in facing the challenges of their specific leadership roles.

Group members may or may not be of the same age or life stage, as the study leads participants to evaluate present challenges and to review earlier experiences in the light of God's Word.

Who Can Lead a *Keeping Your Heart for Ministry* Study?

Any church member — pastor, staff member, lay leader, or Christian school leader — can lead the group. Ideally the leader would be an individual who is sensitive to the needs of others and one who would not be overwhelmed by an emotional response by any member of the group. The leader should treat all discussions as confidential and should display the highest levels of integrity throughout the course of study.

The fact that a person has struggles of his or her own should not in any way discourage that person from leading a group. The ideal leader is a fellow struggler, someone who relates to the issues involved and is perhaps only a little further down the road than the rest of the group members in surrendering every aspect of ministry to God's control.

Group leaders should be convicted about the need to keep one's heart for ministry and willing to share their own experiences transparently. Since the group leader leads by modeling, recruiting leaders who are role models in terms of wholeheartedly giving time, talents, and energies for the Lord's work is important.

Qualities of an Effective Group Leader

What are some traits of an effective group leader? This person—

- Is a growing Christian, a person of prayer, and one who has faith in what God can do.
- Has a commitment to keep private information confidential.
- Is an active member of the sponsoring church.
- Is able to relate well to people.
- Has a knowledge of Scripture.
- Senses God's call to be involved in a ministry to others in the body of Christ.
- Is comfortable in the presence of people who share painful life experiences. In the process of these group discussions, members may reflect on hurtful times when they made wrong choices in their ministry experiences. A person who only feels comfortable when contemporaries are cheerful and upbeat may need to reconsider whether he or she is appropriate to lead a *Keeping Your Heart for Ministry* group.

Skills Needed to Lead a Successful Small-Group Process

What are some skills that a group leader needs? A successful group leader for *Keeping Your Heart for Ministry* will —

- Maintain eye contact as members share. When appropriate, nod your head or use occasional verbal phrases to indicate that you are listening to what someone is saying.
- Use good listening skills. To encourage sharing, make sure you or someone in the group offers some type of response when any group member shares.
- Try to read body language and nonverbal cues. Attempt to draw out people who are, for example, listening intently, withdrawing, or looking as though they are full of pain. Depend on God for sensitivity.
- Affirm strong emotion, such as tears. Phrases such as "I sense a lot of hurt in what you just shared . . . " or "I'm sure that must have been very disappointing" help people put a name to their emotions and validate them.

Notes

Notes

- Avoid allowing one member to dominate discussions. If someone has talked too long, gently try to steer the conversation to someone else. Help the person summarize. Watch for the slightest break in monologue to turn the conversation to someone else. State, "I'm wondering whether anyone else has a thought to share on this subject."
- Steer the group away from advice-giving. Help members share out of their own experience ("Something that has worked for me is . . ." or "Here's what I've learned . . .") instead of prefacing remarks with, "What you should do is . . . ."
- Announce to the group that you will begin and end on time. Begin the group even if all members have not arrived. Demonstrating consistency and orderliness in your life and management of your group can serve as an effective role model in leadership.

Getting Started

Pray. Seek God's direction about conducting a study of *Keeping Your Heart for Ministry* with the group you have identified.

Seek approval. If the study is to be held for members of your church (staff or ministry leadership), discuss your plans with the pastor and/or others who are charged with responsibility for approving such studies. Provide a copy of the book for those who need to evaluate the study goals, process, content, and procedures. If the study is to be held for a group of ministers or denominational leaders, select a group by mutual consent.

Select a group leader. See the section titled, "Who Can Lead a *Keeping Your Heart for Ministry* Study?" Use the section "How to Train Leaders" on pages 125-126 and arrange a training session to prepare the group leader(s).

Establish the time, dates, and place for group sessions. If held in your church, this step requires coordination with the general church calendar. Selecting an unusual time, outside the typical church schedule, generally works best.

Recruit members. Schedule at least a four-week period to register members and promote the group. Use announcements in the church bulletin, bulletin boards, or displays throughout the church to promote the study. Personal testimonies in worship and announcements in Bible study classes or deacons' meetings are other ways to promote the study depending on the makeup of the class. The optimal group size is no more than eight members. This number allows each participant to contribute something during each session. Provide a trained leader for each group.

Order materials. Order a copy of *Keeping Your Heart for Ministry* for each participant at least six weeks prior to the starting date. If couples participate, order a book for both husband and wife.

Set fees. Ask members to purchase their own books unless the church has decided to subsidize the cost. Members should pay at least part of the cost to invest in *Keeping Your Heart for Ministry.*

Determine child care. If child care is needed for your group, decide if you will provide it for group members' children. Providing care may allow some individuals to attend who might not otherwise be able to do so. Perhaps your church would be willing to provide care at no cost if the meetings are held at a time during the week when child care is not normally provided. However, the church could also arrange for care at a nominal cost to members.

How to Train Leaders

- Churches that elect to study *Keeping Your Heart for Ministry* and that will be forming several study groups can benefit from conducting leader training several weeks before the study. After leaders are enlisted, ask them to commit to a two-hour training session to equip them to lead *Keeping Your Heart for Ministry* groups.

- Ask leaders to complete Week 1 of their *Keeping Your Heart for Ministry* member books before attending the training so they will be generally familiar with the concepts and learning approach.

Notes

Notes

- If you have more than eight leaders attending the training session, divide the group and ask another facilitator to lead a separate training for one of the groups while you lead the other one.

- Prepare the meeting room.
  1. Provide a circle of chairs for the number of participants.
  2. Provide pencils for participants.
  3. Prepare name tags, if needed.

- Sample Training Schedule *(2 hours)*
  1. Introduction *(20 minutes)* — Ask participants to introduce themselves to each other if they are not well acquainted. Ask each participant to briefly tell one challenge and one victory he or she has experienced in the area of ministry in which he or she serves.
  2. Describe the plan for the *Keeping Your Heart for Ministry* studies in your church. *(20 minutes)* — Explain the rationale for the church's scheduling the emphasis, the biblical basis, the benefits to the individual participant, and the benefits to the church as a corporate body. Overview the plans that are being made for church preparation, promotion, enlistment, child care, fees, scheduling.
  3. Review the high points of the section "Skills Needed to Lead a Successful Small-Group Process" on page 123 of this *Leader Guide*. Invite questions. *(30 minutes)*
  4. Review the member book design and how to use it. *(30 minutes)* — Explain that the interactive style of the material allows members to read the text and then answer questions that relate to the material members just read. Discuss questions or comments participants have. Review the organization of the leader's material. Direct leaders to the "How Does a Group Session Work?" and "Preparing for a Group Session" segments on pages 127-128 that leaders are to use to prepare for each session. Also direct them to the "After the Session" segment on page 131 to use for review after each session.
  5. Lead the group leaders in conversational prayer for the upcoming groups. *(20 minutes)* — Pray for growth in the lives of individual members and in the life of the church through the *Keeping Your Heart for Ministry* study.

How Does a Group Session Work?

Each session is one hour in length. Time increments for each part of the session are included in the *Leader Guide*. Members are to complete all weekly assignment before the group sessions. Sessions are divided into:

Opening Time
One-on-One Sharing or Small-Group Time
Large-Group Time
Circle of Prayer

During some sessions you may want to substitute small groups of three or four for the one-on-one sharing time, depending on the subject matter under discussion. Using variety will prevent monotony and enhance participation.

Encourage the members to read the Covenant appearing on page 117. Explain the need for conversations within the group to remain private and for each member to respect any confidences shared. Urge members to refrain from mentioning group matters even in well-meaning prayer requests outside the group in which you supply no specific names. Although no names may be mentioned, the circumstances you state may be just enough to cause a non-member to be able to identify the actual situation to which you refer. At that point, confidentiality has been breached, just as though you had stated the name of the person involved. Ask all members to sign each other's books at the end of the first session.

Prepare the assigned room before each session, making certain there are just enough chairs for the group. If possible, prepare name tags in advance if group members do not know each other.

Preparing for a Group Session

Secure copies of *Keeping Your Heart for Ministry* for each member. Make certain that each participant has a copy. **Ask members to read the introduction and to complete the Week 1 work before attending the first group session.** Confirm with each the date, time, and place for sessions. Draw

Notes

Notes

attention to the Covenant on page 117 of their books, and ask them to read it before the first meeting.

Reread "Qualities of an Effective Group Leader" and "Skills Needed to Lead a Successful Small-Group Process" as you prepare your own heart.

Read the book *Keeping Your Heart for Ministry*, including the *Leader Guide* section, before you attempt to lead the study. Complete at least two weekly assignments before beginning the study, and always stay at least one week ahead of the group in completing assignments.

Prepare the assigned room before each session, making certain there are just enough chairs for members. If you are meeting in a home or some other location, contact the hostess or person in charge to confirm room set-up and meeting times. If possible, prepare name tags in advance if group members do not know each other. Take them up at the close of the session and have them ready for the next session.

Find a quiet time and place to pray. Call each member's name, asking the Lord to give you wisdom as you pray and as you lead the session. Ask for sensitivity and understanding during times of sharing.

Review the Group Session for the week you are preparing to lead. Review the interactive work you have done during daily assignments.

Plan to stay within the times allotted for each activity, but keep in mind that sharing is more important than a schedule. Members may wish to "camp" on an event or issue that is important to all group members, and you will want to be sensitive to their needs. Allowing God to work may mean great flexibility in the schedule.

GROUP SESSION 1 *(1 hour)*

Notes

A. Opening Time *(25 minutes)*

1. Welcome each person and give him or her a name tag. As members arrive, introduce them to each other. Let everyone visit informally until time to begin. Remind members to turn in name tags to you after each session. They may pick them up from you at the beginning of each meeting time.
2. Begin promptly. Remind the group that you will begin and end each session on time. If group members want to fellowship or have additional discussions after the session, they may do so, but they can count on you to be prompt.
3. Use the following icebreaker: Ask each person to tell one present victory and one present challenge in his or her area of church responsibility. As leader, share first, as you set the standard for giving concise answers. If you answer the questions in about 45 to 60 seconds, most of the members will also.
4. Call attention to the covenant on page 117 of the member book. Ask whether anyone has questions about the covenant. (Refer to page 127 for the importance of confidentiality.) Ask each member to pass his or her signed covenant to the right so each person can sign the covenant of every member of the group. Explain that praying for group members is an important part of *Keeping Your Heart for Ministry.* Encourage members to refer to the list of members while they are learning names in order to pray for everyone.
5. Explain that just because you are group leader, you have not necessarily mastered all the concepts presented in the material but that you are a fellow struggler who is perhaps just a bit further down the road than are members. Explain that you, like they, will be sharing out of your own pilgrimage toward keeping your heart for the ministry as members discuss their challenges and victories.
6. Kick off the session with a group sharing time. Note that Proverbs 4:23 says you have a responsibility to keep your heart. Ask each member to briefly share his or her first impression of what that means. A later statement in Day 1 describes keeping the heart as a

Notes

"lifelong spiritual responsibility." Ask members how they responded to this statement. Ask a volunteer to tell one specific way a person can maintain this responsibility for keeping the heart.

B. One-on-One Sharing *(10 minutes)*

1. Ask each member to pair off with another member (no spouses). Ask members, within pairs, to share a time they have served with an impure motive. Ask each to share what he or she learned from that experience.
2. Ask each person to share a time he or she served without obvious results.
3. Ask members to return to the large-group format. Ask one volunteer to share one of his or her answers mentioned in the one-on-one setting.

C. Large-Group Time *(20 minutes)*

1. Lead a brief discussion (10 minutes at most) on reprioritizing earthly treasures. Ask members to share their reaction to the story about Bob Harrington (page 13). Ask whether anyone can see himself in any of the circumstances that led to his downfall.
2. Ask someone to tell a special Scripture that has inspired him or her to serve more obediently and with a whole heart.
3. Ask one volunteer to tell about someone like Pastor Harvey (page 32) who has been a role model in that person's life, serving with a heart like God's.
4. Ask, "What activity during this week's study did God use to get your attention and/or move you in a direction He wants for you?" Allow as many as desire to respond in the time available.

D. Circle of Prayer *(5 minutes)*

1. Remind members to pray for each other during the week. Remind them that although what is said in the group is confidential, they can pray privately throughout the week for members' concerns voiced during the group sessions.
2. Close in prayer. Ask each person who is willing to pray a sentence prayer, thanking God for something special he or she learned from this week's study. As leader, begin the prayer time to set the pace for sentence prayers.

After the Session
(Review the following checklist before you conduct each session throughout the *Keeping Your Heart for Ministry* study.)

- ❑ Pray about the events that transpired during the session just concluded. Thank God for His activity in the midst of the session. Ask the Holy Spirit to continue to stir each member's heart during the coming week, so that each can make practical application of lessons learned.
- ❑ Use the following questions to evaluate your leadership.
  - Was I thoroughly prepared?
  - Did I follow the leader guide?
  - Did I provide positive leadership?
  - Was I a servant leader?
  - Did I create a group environment?
  - Did I help members communicate with each other?
  - Do members understand the purpose of the study?
  - Was I enthusiastic about how God will use *Keeping Your Heart for Ministry* in members' lives and in the life of our church?
- ❑ Before the next group session pray specifically for each member.
- ❑ Call and encourage all members in the study of the next week's material. Answer questions they may have, and encourage any who seem to need it. Thank each member for his or her participation.

Notes

Notes

GROUP SESSION 2 *(1 hour)*

A. Opening Time *(10 minutes)*

1. Greet each person as he or she arrives. Be sensitive to difficulties members may be having with completing assignments. Begin promptly.
2. As a get-started activity, invite two or three volunteers to briefly describe a time in their lives when they believe they served God with wholehearted devotion. Ask them to describe what characterized that time — what traits or practices existed. Tell members this can be a current situation or a time past. Start with an example of your own. Be concise, and each member will follow suit. (For example, a leader might say, "The time my wife and I led a neighborhood Bible study is a time I recall serving the Lord wholeheartedly. The two of us prayed daily for each participant. We saw our efforts bear fruit for the Lord.")
3. After the sharing time, conclude this portion with prayer. Ask God to help each group member do whatever is necessary to maintain this type of wholehearted devotion or to attain it once again, if they can't attest to it at the present time in their lives.

B. Small-Group Time *(20 minutes)*

1. Ask members to divide into small groups of three or four persons each. Ask each person in the small groups to discuss their challenges in seeking God with their whole heart. Ask them to review King Jehoshaphat's *actions* (see pages 41-43) to see if there is application for ministry today (2 Chronicles 19:3). Now ask one volunteer per group to discuss within the small groups a time when he or she personally lost heart and what reassured the individual.
2. Ask members to return to the large-group format. Ask for a volunteer who is willing to share with everyone what he or she disclosed in the small-group setting about the volunteer's personal loss of heart and how it was counteracted. Comment to members that as painful as some of our disclosures might be, we benefit from realizing that others in ministry have experienced some of the same challenges. Remind members of God's faithfulness in the midst of difficulty.

C. Large-Group Time *(25 minutes)*

1. Ask members to discuss their experiences and challenges in following God wherever He leads. Ask a volunteer to share about a time when he or she demonstrated a willingness to follow God into a hard or unfruitful ministry.
2. Call on someone to tell what "different spirit," such as personal disciplines, keep them following God (see pages 52-53). Ask another member to tell about personal practices, such as confession or actively avoiding grudges, bad habits, places, or people, that help the person keep a heart for God.
3. Ask, "What activity during this week's study did God use to get your attention and/or move you in a direction He wants for you?" Allow as many as desire to respond in the time available.
4. Thank members for their willingness to be vulnerable before each other. Assure them that this is a safe place to share. Encourage members to lift each other up in prayer during the week as they seek to demonstrate a "different spirit" to others.

D. Circle of Prayer *(5 minutes)*

1. Conclude with a season of silent prayer. Ask members to pray that God will help them remove any obstacle that keeps them from following God with a "different spirit" and a whole heart.
2. After members have prayed silently for a time, as leader conclude with a prayer for the group.

Notes

Notes

GROUP SESSION 3 *(1 hour)*

A. Opening Time *(10 minutes)*

1. Begin the session on time even if all members are not present. Ask for special prayer requests. As leader, begin with a brief prayer.
2. Lead the group in an opening discussion about the various distractions that can occur in ministry. Ask each person to tell one thing or current life circumstance that distracts him or her during ministry tasks. Then ask each to tell a way that the person works to avoid the distraction mentioned and to focus on things above. You share first, and ask members to follow suit. (For example, you might say, "One thing that distracts me in my ministry is my desire to be a people pleaser and to do the popular thing rather than the right thing. I counteract this by asking God to remind me that ultimately only His approval of me matters."

B. One-on-One Sharing *(20 minutes)*

1. Ask members to divide into pairs for today's sharing time. Encourage members to pair off with someone different than in last week's sharing time.
2. Ask members to share within pairs about warning signs they've relied on to indicate their hearts needed purifying. They may desire to refer back to the exercise on pages 60-61 in this week's work and to share some of the items they checked. Ask members to pray for each other that the Holy Spirit will continue to prompt them when they need to be more alert to the condition of their hearts.

C. Large-Group Time *(25 minutes)*

1. Ask members to return to the large-group setting. Ask volunteers to tell about ways they keep a prepared heart. For example, they may desire to share suggestions about times and places they have found workable for their personal quiet times, Scripture passages they find meaningful, or patterns they use to pray through a prayer list.

2. Call on a couple of volunteers to share their experiences with transparency — times in which their willingness to admit character flaws and lessons God taught them have had a positive outcome in their ministry (see pages 72-73). As leader, share first. Your example might be something like, "When I told my discipleship group about how I once took a church job because it flattered my ego instead of because I was trying to obey God, it prompted them to begin sharing about their own lack of obedience."
3. Ask one or two members to share their concept of what it means to be "given the kingdom." (See Week 3 Introduction, Luke 12:32.)
4. Ask, "What activity during this week's study did God use to get your attention and/or move you in a direction He wants for you?" Allow as many as desire to respond in the time available.

D. Circle of Prayer *(5 minutes)*

1. Ask members to pray aloud briefly as they feel led. As leader, you begin and ask others to follow. Suggest that members ask God to deal with them in an area of need He has impressed on their hearts during today's meeting.
2. As the group closes, remind members that you are available to pray with them as personal needs arise.

Notes

Notes

GROUP SESSION 4 *(1 hour)*

A. Opening Time *(10 minutes)*

1. Greet members as they arrive. Inquire about answers to prayer requests that have been mentioned during the time the group has met together. Stop and thank God for these; ask His guidance and blessing on the meeting time.
2. Ask a couple of volunteers to tell one way they try to stay attuned to the spiritual condition of those they serve and ways they observe spiritual transformation in others. Ask one or two persons to share a story of a transformed life — someone from their own church experience. Be prepared to share first, and others will follow.

B. Small-Group Time *(20 minutes)*

Ask members to again form small groups of three or four members each. Ask members to discuss times in which they have felt genuinely brokenhearted for those they serve. Ask members if they have any observations about why they were especially open and sensitive to these needs and concerns during that time. (For example, a group member might say, "I was especially attuned to my committee member's brokenness because I had been a good listener when she was telling about her painful childhood." After about 15 minutes of sharing, ask one member of each group to say a prayer within the small group for the concerns voiced by group members, praying specifically that group members would keep a spirit of brokenness about them as they minister.

C. Large-Group Time *(25 minutes)*

1. Ask members to return to the large-group setting. Choose from among these questions for your large-group discussion:

   - Ask a volunteer to share one way he or she works to maintain sound relationships with those the person serves.
   - Ask a volunteer to tell about someone with whom he or she worked who matured in Christ as a result of time spent with the person.

- Ask a volunteer to tell about how he or she sacrifices for the group (Sunday School class, prayer ministry, committee, congregation, etc.) the person serves, beyond the mere giving of time in a leadership role.

2. Remember to share any experience you, as leader, have had in these areas. Heartily congratulate members on victories achieved.
3. Ask, "What activity during this week's study did God use to get your attention and/or move you in a direction He wants for you?" Allow as many as desire to respond in the time available.

D. Circle of Prayer *(5 minutes)*

1. Thank members for their participation in this session. Remind members to pray for each other throughout the week.
2. Close in a circle of prayer. Ask members to think of one person within the scope of his or her ministry with whom he or she would like a relationship to be better. Ask members to pray silently that God would remove any barrier to a healthy, Christlike relationship. After a few minutes of silent prayer, close by asking God's blessings on members as they study the concluding week's work.

Notes

Notes

GROUP SESSION 5 *(1 hour)*

A. Opening Time *(10 minutes)*

As a get-started activity, ask a couple of volunteers to tell one way in which the world has been on their hearts in the past week. Ask a member to comment on the statement in the Week 5 Introduction, "God has sent you on a rescue mission." Remind members that grief for the lost world characterized Christ's earthly ministry and is what He wants their ministries to be about, also. Add your own testimony to the sharing time. Call on a volunteer who might be willing to voice an opening prayer for the concerns mentioned.

B. One-on-One Sharing *(25 minutes)*

1. As members divide into pairs for one-on-one sharing time, ask members to refer to their workbooks to the exercise on pages 94-95 under the heading, "Grief for Hard-Hearted People." Ask them to share which of the statements they checked (or anything they wrote under "other") that characterizes ways they find themselves performing ministry with a heart hardened to the lost condition of others.
2. As members reconvene into the large group, call on someone who might be willing to share what he or she confessed in the one-on-one time. Confess your own weakness in this regard. Possibly some intense struggles and past mistakes have been shared during this time of hearing each others' experiences. Suggest that members bow their heads and pray silently for themselves and for each other — that God would empower everyone present to have a genuine heart for those who need the gospel.

C. Large-Group Time *(20 minutes)*

1. In the large group, refer members back to the Week-5 example of the day care center director who treated the church badly (see page 112). Ask a member who might be willing to share a similar experience.
2. Ask members to share ways in which they feel motivated to take concrete action regarding the world's lostness. Try to encourage each member to share some new commitment he or she, as a result

of this week's work, may have made regarding being on mission to a lost world. (Possible comments might be: "I am more committed than ever to pray for missionaries who are on the prayer list" or "I feel God leading me to sign up for a volunteer mission trip this summer.") Be sure to add your own testimony to those of the participants.

3. Ask two members to share the impact the Week 5 study has had on their lives.

Notes

D. Circle of Prayer *(5 minutes)*

1. Thank members for the privilege of leading them in this course. Congratulate them on completing their study of *Keeping Your Heart for Ministry.* Assure them that the time investment they have made in learning to keep their hearts for ministry will make their Christian walk more meaningful in the days ahead. Commit to pray for them and their ministries in the ensuing days. Encourage members to pray for each other and for you as God empowers each person to apply the precepts of the study.
2. Ask each member to pray aloud for the person on his or her right — that the Lord will help that person keep the "on-mission" commitment just voiced. As leader, close the prayer time, thanking God for the time the group has spent together and for lessons learned. Ask God to help you and each member to keep his or her heart for ministry.

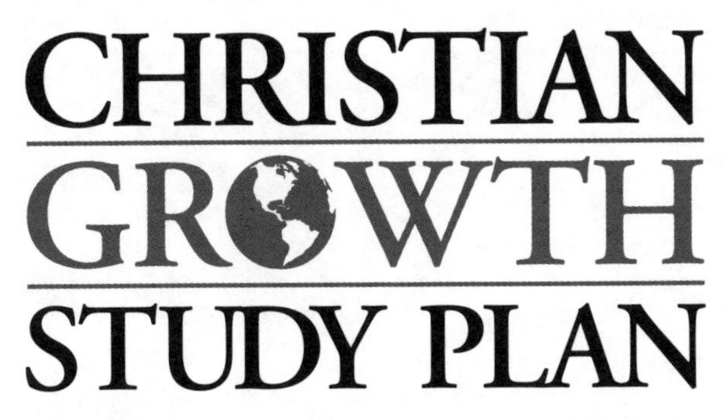

Preparing Christians to Serve

In the **Christian Growth Study Plan (formerly Church Study Course)**, this book ***KEEPING YOUR HEART FOR MINISTRY*** is a resource for course credit in the subject area **Ministry** of the Christian Growth category and two courses in **Leadership and Skill Development** diploma plans. To receive credit, read the book, complete the learning activities, show your work to your pastor, a staff member, or church leader, then complete the information on the next page. The form may be duplicated. Send the completed page to:

Christian Growth Study Plan
127 Ninth Avenue, North, MSN 117
Nashville, TN 37234-0117
FAX: (615)251-5067

For information about the Christian Growth Study Plan, refer to the current Christian Growth Study Plan Catalog. Your church office may have a copy. If not, request a free copy from the Christian Growth Study Plan office (615/251-2525).

KEEPING YOUR HEART FOR MINISTRY

Please check the appropriate box indicating the diploma you want to apply credit. You may check more than one:

- ❑ CG - 0667 Ministry
- ❑ LS - 0078 Pastoral Ministry
- ❑ LS - 0250 Childhood Education (Church Leadership)

PARTICIPANT INFORMATION

Social Security Number (USA ONLY)	Personal CGSP Number*	Date of Birth (MONTH, DAY, YEAR)
_ _ _ – _ _ – _ _ _ _	_ _ _ _ – _ _ _ – _ _ _	_ _ – _ _ – _ _

Name (First, Middle, Last)	Home Phone
	_ _ _ – _ _ _ – _ _ _ _

Address (Street, Route, or P.O. Box)	City, State, or Province	Zip/Postal Code

CHURCH INFORMATION

Church Name		
Address (Street, Route, or P.O. Box)	**City, State, or Province**	**Zip/Postal Code**

CHANGE REQUEST ONLY

☐ Former Name		
☐ Former Address	City, State, or Province	Zip/Postal Code
☐ Former Church	City, State, or Province	Zip/Postal Code

Signature of Pastor, Conference Leader, or Other Church Leader	Date

*New participants are requested but not required to give SS# and date of birth. Existing participants, please give CGSP# when using SS# for the first time. Thereafter, only one ID# is required. **Mail to:** Christian Growth Study Plan, 127 Ninth Ave., North, Nashville, TN 37234-0117. Fax: (615)251-5067

Rev. 6-99